D0920693

THE ROOTS OF FAITH

BOOK 1 *God Gives His Word*

Pilot Edition

Under the direction of:

The Reverend Leo G. Henry
Chairman, Diocesan Association of
    Religion Teachers
Pittsburgh, Pennsylvania

Sister Mary Michael Glenn, C.D.P.
Supervisor, Religious Education of the
    Diocese of Pittsburgh
Pittsburgh, Pennsylvania

Contributors:

Sister M. Fidelia, C.S.S.F.
St. Louis School
Cleveland Heights, Ohio

Sisters of Notre Dame de Namur
Massachusetts Province
Ipswich, Massachusetts

Consultants:

The Reverend Gerard S. Sloyan
Catholic University of America
Washington, D.C.

The Reverend John L. Elias
Bethlehem Catholic High School
Bethlehem, Pennsylvania

 HARCOURT, BRACE & WORLD, INC.

New York • Chicago • San Francisco • Atlanta • Dallas

Nihil Obstat: William J. Winter
                    CENSOR LIBRORUM

Imprimatur: ✠ Vincent M. Leonard
                    AUXILIARY BISHOP OF PITTSBURGH

June 19, 1966

The Nihil Obstat and Imprimatur are official declarations that a book or pamphlet is free of doctrinal or moral error. No implication is contained therein that those who have granted the Nihil Obstat and Imprimatur agree with the contents, opinions, or statements expressed.

Copyright © 1966 by Harcourt, Brace & World, Inc.

All rights reserved. No part of this publication may be reproduced or transmitted in any form or by any means, electronic or mechanical, including photocopy, recording, or any information storage and retrieval system, without permission in writing from the publisher.

Printed in the United States of America

COVER: The figure design by Sister M. Roberta, D.D.R., shows many persons united in their work for Christ. Their attitudes represent a broad range of human activities and experiences: praise, love, prayer, service, labor, sleep, joy, and suffering.

The illustrations in the book were done by
Sister M. Roberta, D.D.R.; Sister M. Alene, C.D.P.;
and Sister M. Jane, C.S.S.F.

ACKNOWLEDGMENTS: For permission to reprint copyrighted material, grateful acknowledgment is made to the following publishers, authors, and agents:

TEXT

AMERICA PRESS: From *Mater et Magistra* by Pope John XXIII.

BIBLICA, BRUGES, BELGIUM: The text in the art work on pp. 37 and 56, and the prayer on p. 69 from *St. Andrew Bible Missal*, edited by the Missal Commission, St. Andrew's Abbey.

THE BRUCE PUBLISHING COMPANY: From *The Two Commandments of Christ* by McGarrigle.

CATHOLIC ACTION FEDERATIONS AND REV. LEO T. MAHON: From *Apostolate* Magazine, Spring, 1964, by the Priests of San Miguelito.

THE CONFRATERNITY OF CHRISTIAN DOCTRINE, NATIONAL CENTER: The text of the Scriptures herein from the Confraternity version of *The Holy Bible*. From "God Speaks with College Students in Bible Services" by Rev. Robert W. Case, O.S.B., from *The Living Light*, Summer, 1964.

DESCLEE CO., INC.: From *Christian Commitment to God and to the World* by Robert Guelluy, published by Desclee Co., Inc., New York, 1965.

WALTER DURIG: From "The Eucharist as Symbol of the Consecration of the World" by Walter Durig in *The Christian and the World*, edited by Karl Rahner.

F.E.L. CHURCH PUBLICATIONS: "All of My Life" and "My Lord Is Long A Comin'" by Sister Germaine from *Hymnal for Young Christians*, copyright © 1966 by F.E.L. Church Publications.

FIDES PUBLISHERS: From *The Meaning of Success* by Michel Quoist. From the *Constitution on the Church*, National Catholic Laymen's Retreat Conference Edition. From *New Horizons* by Barnabas Ahern.

BROTHER VAL HABJAN, S.M.: "I Shall Be Your God" and "Fear Not" by Brother Val Habjan, S.M., North Catholic High School, Pittsburgh, Pennsylvania.

HARCOURT, BRACE & WORLD, INC.: From *Complete Poems and Plays, 1909-1950* by T. S. Eliot.

HELICON PRESS, INC.: From *The Wide World, My Parish* by Yves Congar, O.P. All rights reserved.

HOLT, RINEHART AND WINSTON, INC.: From "Revelation" from *Complete Poems of Robert Frost*, copyright 1934 by Holt, Rinehart and Winston, Inc.; © 1962 by Robert Frost. From *Jesus Christ: Our Life and Worship* by Vincent Novak, S.J., copyright 1965.

LITURGICAL PRESS: From *The Men and the Message of the Old Testament* by P. Ellis.

GRETCHEN MEYER: "Take," and "David," by Gretchen Meyer.

THE NEWMAN PRESS: From *That Man Is You* by Louis Evely. From *The Christian Approach to the Bible* by Charlier.

THE NEWMAN PRESS AND GEOFFREY CHAPMAN LIMITED: From *Lay People in the Church* by Yves Congar, published in the U.S.A. and in England.

NEWSWEEK, INC.: From "He Had That Special Grace—in So Many Ways" by Benjamin Bradlee in *Newsweek*, December 2, 1963, copyright © 1963 by Newsweek, Inc.

PAULIST PRESS: From *Presence of God* by G. Tavard. From *Who Is God?* by Reginald McCurdy. From *Death For a Christian* by Stanley B. Marrow. From *The Liturgy Constitution*.

PRENTICE-HALL, INC.: The excerpt on p. 47 and the chart on pp. 194-195 from *Approaches to the Bible: The Old Testament* by Aldo J. Tos, © 1963. From *The Israel of God* by John M. Oesterreicher, © 1963.

RANDOM HOUSE, INC.: From *The Family and the Bible* by Mary Reed Newland, copyright © 1963 by Mary Reed Newland.

HENRY REGNERY COMPANY: From *To Live Is Christ,* Volume I, Teacher's Manual by Brother J. Frederick, F.S.C., and Brother H. Albert, F.S.C., copyright 1965 by Henry Regnery Company.

REVIEW FOR RELIGIOUS: "Let Us Give Thanks to the Lord Our God" by Carl Pfeifer, S.J., from *Review for Religious,* Vol. 20 (1961), p, 401.

SCEPTER PUBLISHERS: From *The Essence of Christianity* by M. Schmaus.

CHARLES SCRIBNER'S SONS: From *The Wind in the Willows* by Kenneth Grahame.

SHEED & WARD INC.: From *The Christian Commitment* by Karl Rahner, © 1963 by Sheed & Ward, Ltd.

THE VIKING PRESS, INC.: From "Conversation in Avila" from *Times Three* by Phyllis McGinley, copyright 1954 by Phyllis McGinley. From "The Creation" from *God's Trombones* by James Weldon Johnson, copyright 1927 by The Viking Press, Inc.; renewed © 1955 by Grace Nail Johnson.

THE WESTMINSTER PRESS: From *The Bible Speaks to You* by Robert McAfee Brown, copyright 1955 by W. L. Jenkins.

PICTURES, MAPS, AND ILLUSTRATIONS

BUCHMAN: Pp. 81, 101, 135, and 147.

HILL'S STUDIO: Pp. 8, 24, 27, 28, and 62.

PRENTICE-HALL, INC.: The map on p. 113 adapted from *Approaches to the Bible: The Old Testament* by Aldo J. Tos, © 1963.

CHARLES SCRIBNER'S SONS: The illustration on p. 90 adapted from *Augustus Caesar's World* by Genevieve Foster. Copyright 1947 by Genevieve Foster.

SISTER M. ROBERTA, D.D.R.: The maps on pp. 31 and 50 by Sister M. Roberta, D.D.R.

UNITED PRESS INTERNATIONAL: P. 76.

JOSEPH F. WAGNER, INC.: The map on p. 74 adapted from *The Catholic Biblical Encyclopedia*.

FOREWORD

The chapter headings of this new religion book may well be jarring, if not unintelligible to my generation, i.e., the generation of many of the pastors, teachers, and parents of the students for whom the book is intended.

This will be further proof that the book is precisely the type of book likely to prove acceptable to the students and to have the desired effect in communicating to them the heart of the Christian creed and moral code.

Our young people talk a language different from that of the generation of their fathers; their catch-phrases, slogans, battle cries, and figures of speech are not those of a generation ago. Because the superficial patterns of life which provide our figures of speech and condition our phrases are different from those of earlier generations, it is not surprising that modes of expression should so change that one generation finds obscure, in their wording at least, propositions that make all manner of sense to another.

However, the underlying truths remain the same. So do the ultimate needs, spiritual and intellectual, of students. So does the essential message of the teaching Church. And so, the substance of this up-to-date book, couched in modern language intelligible to contemporary young people, remains the truths of the unchanging Gospel, the faith of the Eternal Church, ever ancient, ever new.

In addition to having a style that is fresh and contemporary, this book has other important qualities which commend it to the teacher, school administrator, or parent. Its use of Sacred Scripture, its Christian personalist emphasis, its practical concerns—all help to mirror the authentic spirit of Vatican Council II. So also is its value enhanced by the ready and natural relationship it achieves between liturgy and life, between art and instruction, between theory and practice in Christian living.

I therefore commend it to all those charged with the holy responsibility of choosing textbooks for the instruction of the generation coming along. If they really wish to share the "big idea" of the faith that has meant so much to us, to make friends for God among young people and to guarantee the natural development and supernatural perfection of those whom chiefly they love, the young people preparing to take our places in the Church and the world, they will find this book (and the series of which it is a part) an attractive, effective instrument for their purposes.

Faithfully in Christ,

The Most Reverend John Wright
Bishop of Pittsburgh

CONTENTS

Prologue

It's the King of Understatements to say that writing an open letter is difficult. How to address you sincerely poses the first problem. To be called "girls and boys" puts you back in grade school; "teenagers" implies: Read this now, forget it later; "friends" is untrue yet, and socially unreal; "students" or "pupils" infers your being reached mainly on an academic level, not as a whole person; "kids"...well? Do you see why the only appropriate greeting is of St. Paul? Considering our mutual relationship to God and His Son Jesus Christ, you can only be . . .

Dear Brothers and Sisters,

Welcome to high school! Welcome to this book meant to serve you. The doors were open --this book is open--and we hope you come with an open mind and heart. With this openness which is a vastness, God can reveal Himself to you. But you will see only what you want to see. If you desire the vision that will make your life worth living, your religion class can help you find yourself and God and others...and live according to those findings!

It isn't stupid to say "find yourself." We're all a little way out or too far in, out of bounds or wrapped up tight. We're never quite grown up enough (ever!) to stop playing "Hide and Seek." We play it whenever we want to get away from others, or we live the game. And sometimes we do it to get away from ourselves.

It's Robert Frost who warns us:

"So all who hide too well away
Must speak and tell us where they are."
from "Revelation" by Robert Frost

We don't mean to be sneaky in hiding; frankly we fear the unknown and we run away, or we don't want to be hurt, or we want attention in being sought. Let's be true and in the open even though it may be dark, for that's when we show what we really are. Let's find our real selves and develop that self fully. And where do we look? In God, in others, in the depth of our own persons.

It might be consoling to hear Isaiah the prophet say that God is a hidden God.   There's adventure here.   There's action!   Let's hunt for this God and find Him, for He hides that we may have the joy of finding Him.

Then let us find one another. This can be done by openness in discussion, being ready to speak and ready to listen to others, by having a real concern for them. You know, minds are like para- chutes; they only function when open. Some of us may find this game of life pretty rugged, and if we can help, why not? Let's help one another to the goal, **not a telephone pole, or a lamp post, or a chestnut tree,** but a life which leads to a Person, THE PERSON who is looking for us and respects our freedom in going to Him.

Chapter 1 -
God's Plan of Salvation in Christ

A Freshman Once Said
What's the big idea?

"I wish I could skip being a freshman and start high school as a sophomore. There are so many new things to remember, where and when to go, and what books to take. It's very confusing! I feel like the center on the football team who doesn't know the signals and isn't sure where the goal posts are. And to make it worse, I hardly recognize myself--I seem like an altogether different person. What happened to me? It's difficult to believe that I'm the same guy that captained the Safety Patrol so efficiently last year." And Peggy, another freshman, said: "I wonder if I'll ever have the casual grace and self-confidence that the senior girls take so much for granted. I feel completely lost."

1. Why do freshmen feel so insecure?

2. What could be done to improve their situation?

The History of You

Perhaps you too feel that "time is marching on" and sweeping you in its tide. It's a great adventure, but sometimes it's frightening. It's an adventure because you have entered the stream of events and persons that is creating and shaping history. It is frightening because you seem to have been cut off from the past and are not yet able to grasp the future. You are floating around without a chart or rudder in the Sea of the Present. Maybe it will reassure you to know that--

The Past Is in the Present

In some way, the moment of "now" contains all the fullness of the past--your past history is a vital part of your PRESENT self.

3. In what ways is your past present to you now?

4. Draw a line to represent your life-span up to the present date. Place the year of your birth at the beginning and a question mark at the end.

                                         Today
19?_____/_____20?

What chain of events and persons has been shaping your life? Place these along the time line. What relation does each event have to the next?

The Future Is in the Present

In some sense, the future is already touching you today. Your present moment is already enriched.

5. Ruth Ann, a bride-to-be, receives a letter from her sweetheart overseas...."I am coming home soon...Can hardly wait to see you...Get all the plans ready for the wedding.... All my love...Joe." Suddenly her world is transformed. Everything is seen in a new light. Housework, formerly a chore, is now done with lighthearted eagerness. Relations with people are colored by warmth and enthusiasm. The work involved by multiple preparations becomes surprisingly easy. Everything assumes the characteristics of a joyous adventure. In what sense is the promise of Ruth Ann's future already realized?

6. Dave, a high school senior in a small town, has big plans for his future but no money to realize them. His dreams include education at a first-class university, overseas study about the problems of underdeveloped countries, and finally a position with the United Nations. Some months before graduation Dave receives a grant from the United States Government. The amount of money contained in the grant is more than sufficient to make his dreams come true. In what way is the promise of Dave's future already realized?

7. Give some examples of how the future is present to you today?

4

He's Got the Whole World in His Hands

But all our individual histories are a part of a much greater history. To get some idea of the immensity of that history, imagine yourself in the year 2000 vacationing on the moon or on some distant outer-space planet. You want to send a card with the traditional "Having a wonderful time. Wish you were here" to your folks back home. You would send it via SPACE MAIL and the address would look something like this:

NAME:

STREET:

CITY:

STATE:

COUNTRY:

CONTINENT:

PLANET:

GALAXY:

If you watched the films taken by the astronauts in outer space you must have been impressed by the vast reaches of the universe. How did you feel when you got this glimpse into infinity? You must have suspected that its ordered magnificence is part of a tremendous design, and you wondered where "insignificant little you" fit into the picture.

You're not really as insignificant as your comparative size would suggest. In fact, God, our Father, has a "Grand Design" which is directed toward bringing everything and everyone He made to perfect fulfillment. This design is called the History of Salvation, and your own personal history, for better or for worse, is an essential part of that design.

The Grand Design

You have heard the old saying that "history repeats itself." Ancient people,who did not know God,saw history as a circle--a meaningless repetition of similar events. Buddhists call this circle Karma, or Fate, and they keep reaching outside the circle for the Secret of Life,which will break the circle and release them from their treadmill existence.

8. *What patterns have you noticed that are repeated over and over in human history?*

Some moderns see history as a spiral--each revolution takes place on a slightly higher plane as man gets better and better.

9. *Do you agree with this concept of history? Give examples from your study of history to support your statement.*

Christians and Jews believe that after centuries of man's unsuccessful attempts to find God in nature, God took things into His own hands and made contact with man in history. He broke into the circle of man's aimless existence and gave it direction by His saving acts. The circle of history became a line of connected events in which God and man work together to hammer out the details that will eventually form a perfect design. God often has to rework the pattern to erase man's blunders, but the partnership goes on and God never loses patience.

10. *What is the difference between secular history and sacred history?*

His Story Is History

But God's plan is not a THING, it is a PERSON. God's greatest saving act is the Incarnation and in His Son Jesus Christ the perfect design of God comes into existence. The plan continues in the Church as men of every generation make their contribution to the "Grand Design" which will emerge in all its perfection at the Second Coming of Christ.

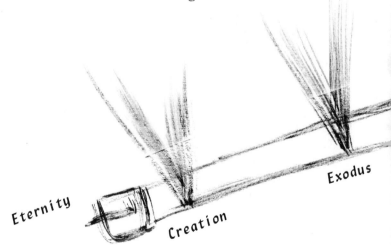

Eternity   Creation   Exodus

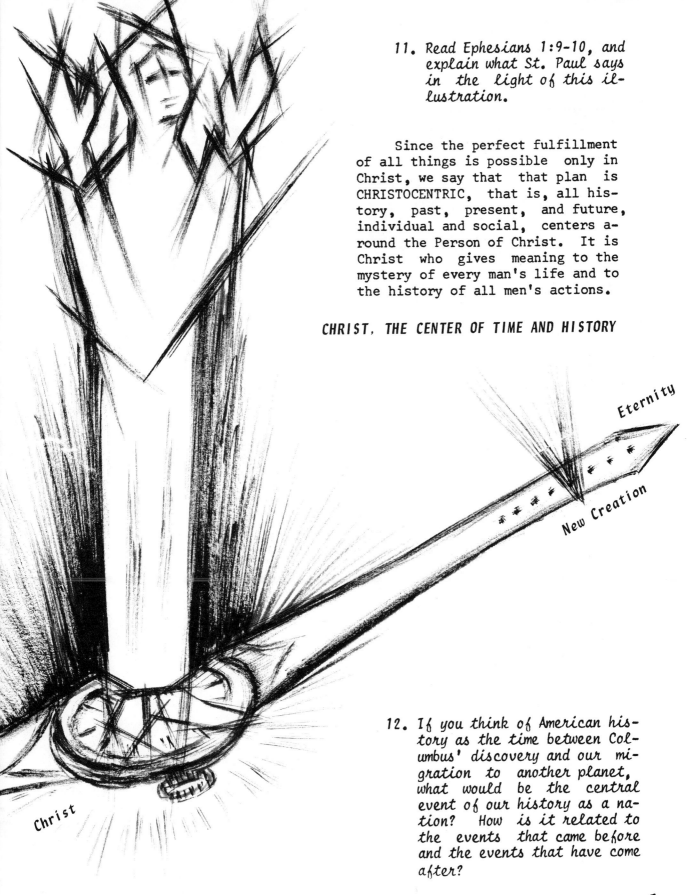

Christ

11. Read Ephesians 1:9-10, and explain what St. Paul says in the light of this illustration.

Since the perfect fulfillment of all things is possible only in Christ, we say that that plan is CHRISTOCENTRIC, that is, all history, past, present, and future, individual and social, centers around the Person of Christ. It is Christ who gives meaning to the mystery of every man's life and to the history of all men's actions.

CHRIST, THE CENTER OF TIME AND HISTORY

Eternity

New Creation

12. If you think of American history as the time between Columbus' discovery and our migration to another planet, what would be the central event of our history as a nation? How is it related to the events that came before and the events that have come after?

Christ, who
came in
history,

continues

to come
in mystery

and will
finally
come in

majesty...

Come, Lord
Jesus!

The Pattern

All of God's saving acts have the same pattern. In each of them a very critical situation becomes the occasion of passing from unfulfillment to fulfillment.

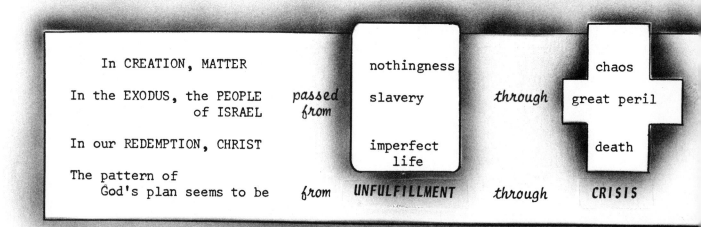

In CREATION, MATTER		nothingness		chaos
In the EXODUS, the PEOPLE of ISRAEL	passed from	slavery	through	great peril
In our REDEMPTION, CHRIST		imperfect life		death
The pattern of God's plan seems to be	from	UNFULFILLMENT	through	CRISIS

13. Read John 12:23-26. When was Jesus' hour? Why did He call this the time to be glorified? What does it mean to be fruitful?

14. Read Rom. 6:4-11. How is baptism a sign of passing through death to a new life? How should the pattern work out in our lives?

Stop Going in Circles!

For some men today, life is still a circle; but for a Christian, life, like a line, has direction. For him, God speaks in His saving acts, which lead to a climax. His history, too, being centered in Christ, looks both backward and forward.

order and life

to   freedom

new and more perfect life

to   FULFILLMENT

Backward...

We look backward because only those who are familiar with the patterns and currents in the past are capable of moving ahead with direction toward the future. To fit into the patterns, we need to be persons who are familiar with the WAYS of the Lord, persons who have a FEEL for the way God does things. God's plan of action is contained in Scripture. We study the Bible because it helps us to understand the past, the present, and the future.

Grow old along with me!
The best is yet to be,
The last of life, for which the first was made:
Our times are in His hand
Who saith, "A whole I planned,
Youth shows but half; trust God: see all, nor be afraid!"
from "Rabbi Ben Ezra" by Robert Browning

... And Forward

Christianity is a religion not only of the PAST but more, it is a faith which participates totally in the PRESENT and is directed wholly toward a FUTURE. The future should be like a magnet attracting us. We need to think about it just as the Israelites wandering in the desert for forty years dreamed of the PROMISED LAND.

15. The measure of a man's greatness can be determined by his vision of a goal. Show how the hope of a football victory determines what you will do to attain this goal. Give other examples of how a goal determines action.

"The Kingdom will be a world that is RECONCILED, for the perfect order IN GOD will pour out a perfect order among things, a harmony that will spread to the tiniest realities."
--Y. Congar, LAY PEOPLE IN THE CHURCH

The Promised Land for the Christian is not simply heaven. When Christ comes again at the Parousia (Second Coming) there will be the Kingdom of God in all its fullness. There will be a NEW HEAVEN and a NEW EARTH.

16. Read Romans 8:18-22. Will this earth be destroyed or changed on that day?

Christ in an era of truth and love, of justice and mercy and peace will come to be the fulfillment of the world's history. And in that fulfillment each man will find his personal fulfillment.

Matthew (13:44-46) tells us that the kingdom of heaven is like a man who found a treasure. He was so fascinated, changed by what he saw, that he sold all. To look into the future gives us COURAGE to be able to LIVE, to LOVE the wonderful things of earth, to be a WHOLE human being.

The Time Is Now!

But this NEW CREATION for which we long is already present and active in the world. St. Paul speaks of it as having already begun at Christ's resurrection and as having begun in us.

> 17. *2 Corinthians 5:17-18. Since when are we "in Christ"? What things still need to be reconciled in our present world? Will this come about as a result of man's effort or as an intervention of God?*
>
> 18. *Ephesians 2:19-22. How does Paul show that Christ is the center of salvation history? How does he show that salvation is a process that has been begun but is not yet completed?*
>
> 19. *V-E Day was a decisive victory in World War II which irreversibly turned the tide of the conflict. However, although the enemy was beaten, he was not disarmed. Many days of battle lay ahead before the final triumph came. How is this situation similar to the establishment of God's Kingdom?*

The Kingdom of God, already present as a REALITY, appears in Christ. **Wherever** Christ is present, there is the Kingdom, but its glory is HIDDEN. The Risen Body of Christ, the New Life, the resurrection powers, and the whole reality of the Kingdom **are now covered**, hidden, wrapped in mysterious action--THE LITURGY--through which its power comes to me.

Your History Is Mystery

Your own particular history is rooted in God's total redemptive plan. And so you see, even though you feel isolated and free-wheeling, even though you are merely a freshman to everybody else, to God you are a very important SOMEBODY with whom He is in partnership to redeem the world.

Your history began in Baptism when you were joined to Christ and so introduced into His "dying" and "rising" and given a pledge of future glory in the gift of the Spirit. It continues in Him through the sacraments and will come to a glorious climax in His victory at the Second Coming.

> 20. *Read Luke 24:13-35. Reflect upon the very personal way in which Christ meets those who are His. What evidence do you find of His concern? What effect did His presence have on them? In what ways is His coming to these disciples similar to how He comes to us?*

Reflection

I AM THE WAY, Christ said. "He is a way different from any other in the world of man. His way leads OUT OF HISTORY and the universe. It leads to a reality beyond time and the cosmos. Christ does not merely show the way: HE IS HIMSELF THE ROAD. Man walks that road in faith. Laying hold on Christ in faith, he puts himself on the road to the Father. Christ is man's only way to the Father and to fulfillment of His own being."

--M. Schmaus, ESSENCE OF CHRISTIANITY

It's Your Move

1. How does the present contain both the past and the future?

2. What is the aim of God's "Grand Design?"

3. Why is the Christian and Jewish concept of religion best illustrated by a straight line?

4. Show how God's plan for mankind is not a thing, but a person. How is Christ in each of the different phases of the plan?

5. What is the underlying pattern of all God's saving acts?

6. What is your interest as a Christian in the past? in the present? in the future?

7. Since the Kingdom is present, but hidden, how does its power come to us?

8. In the light of salvation history, what new meaning is given to your life?

Let Us Give Thanks to the Lord Our God

God's plan of salvation,
   begun in the Jewish nation,
   climaxed in the
      Incarnation and
      Redemption of Christ
continues on to us through
   the Mystical Body of Christ,
   the Church.

By pertaining to this Body
God's saving actions
can reach us in Christ.

Through membership in the
   NEW PEOPLE OF GOD
   we are in personal contact
   with our
      REDEEMER.

His word is proclaimed
   in our midst,
His grace is shared with us
   in our personal encounters
   with Him in His sacraments.
Through our union with Him
   we are enabled to offer
   our Father a suitable
   thank offering, the MASS.

Through our ever-increasing
share in His Life, we have
already a beginning of that
glory which awaits us
with Him in heaven.

And all of this, prefigured in
God's relationships with His
                  chosen people
Is a completely free gift of our
                  Father.

--Carl Pfeifer, S.J.

Chapter 2 -
God's Three-Dimensional Word

A Freshman Once Said
How do I make a friend?

"How can I feel so alone in such a mob? Hundreds of people pass me in the halls every day. Some of them even talk to me, on the bus, in the cafeteria, between classes. But it's all kind of phony. I never say what I'm really thinking and I get the impression that they don't either. I don't mean that we are deliberately lying to each other. It's just that we're all on the surface. Our hearts are not in it. Tell me, how do you really connect with the people you meet every day?"

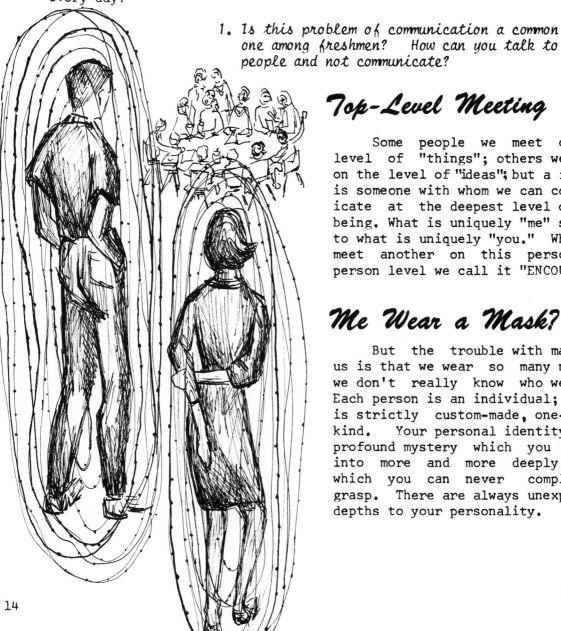

1. *Is this problem of communication a common one among freshmen? How can you talk to people and not communicate?*

Top-Level Meeting

Some people we meet on the level of "things"; others we meet on the level of "ideas"; but a friend is someone with whom we can communicate at the deepest level of our being. What is uniquely "me" speaks to what is uniquely "you." When we meet another on this person-to-person level we call it "ENCOUNTER."

Me Wear a Mask?

But the trouble with many of us is that we wear so many masks, we don't really know who we are. Each person is an individual; each is strictly custom-made, one-of-a-kind. Your personal identity is a profound mystery which you enter into more and more deeply, but which you can never completely grasp. There are always unexplored depths to your personality.

When you meet others in this personal way, you gradually come to know who you are and what you really stand for. That's why friends are so important. They are people to whom you can reveal what you think and feel and in so doing come to discover your true self. God, who made you, holds the whole secret of your person, and your encounters with Him help you most to become what you are. He calls the hidden self into being and He sees a man's true self and helps him to realize it.

Will the Real "You" Please Stand Up

2. *Find an example in the Gospel where an encounter with Christ brought out unsuspected good in the person. Perhaps, there is someone you know whom you can "re-create" by your friendship.*

A Two-Way Street

Encounter is established by a mutual self-revelation and there are some traffic laws on this two-way street.

a. Self-revelation is essentially free. You can know <u>about</u> a person without his consent, but you cannot <u>know</u> the person unless he chooses to reveal himself to you.

3. *If a new boy moves in next door to you, how can you get to* <u>know about</u> *him? How can you get to* <u>know</u> *him?*

b. Self-revelation springs from love and seeks for union. When you disclose the secret of yourself to another, you hope that the other will respond in like manner and thus establish a bond of friendship.

4. *Can you match correctly these effects with their appropriate causes?*

EMOTION   ADMIRATION   LUST   LOVE

"If your heart beats violently when he's around, it's _____ "
"If you want nothing more than to neck with her, it's _____ "
"If you enjoy his brilliant conversation, it's _____ "
"If you want to put all you are at her disposal, it's _____ "

c. Self-revelation happens through signs. The core of self always remains a mystery even to self. Unless you find ways to express yourself (language, gestures, smiles, etc.), you cannot communicate with the other.

God's Signs

God is a Person and we come to know Him in the same kind of encounter by which we meet other living persons. But we will never know Him unless He chooses to reveal Himself to us. When He wants to tell us who He is and what He wills to do, He also must use signs. In order to reveal Himself He uses:

a. Historical Events

- God meets man in the midst of his every-day activity. We can study about God in solitude and seclusion, but it is in the actual human situation that we come to know Him. The events that occur in the world around us, the incidents that happen in our own lives, bring us into contact with God. When the Israelites finally escaped from Pharaoh's army, they recognized God at work in their deliverance. When, 700 years later, they were defeated by the Babylonians and taken into exile, they saw in this tragedy God revealing to them the consequences of their infidelity to the covenant. When Christ was born, the angels came to the shepherds engaged in their ordinary occupation of watching the sheep.

5. Have you ever met God revealing Himself to you in the ordinary events of your life?

b. Persons

- When God acts in history He gives to certain individuals special insight to interpret those events. Men of ardent faith, Abraham, Moses, and the prophets, bore witness to God acting and proclaiming His will and purpose in their particular situations.

6. Who most perfectly expressed God's love for us and His design for friendship with men? Cf. Hebrews 1:1-2. Why is He called "the Word of God"?

c. The Life of a Community

- Since God's words and actions are addressed to all men, He fashioned a People to whom He committed His message and whose duty it was to preserve and transmit the message and to bear witness to its reality by their lives. God continues to speak and act, to reveal Himself through all ages in His people, who are the visible sign of His invisible presence in the world.

7. To what people was God's message committed in the Old Testament? In the New Testament?

8. The American people keep alive the tradition of democracy that they received from the Founding Fathers of our country. How do they do this?

d. A Book

- Moved by the power and spirit of God, men made written records of the truths the people believed and lived by. These writings took many forms: history, short stories, drama, poetry, legal codes, letters, sermons, and philosophic treatises. Gradually these writings, which the people recognized as authentic expressions of their traditions, were collected, edited, and re-edited, and cherished as sacred—the Book for which God was directly responsible. Thus was born the Bible.

"Biblical writers wrote as other men do and left the imprint of their personality on their work. For the most part, they were not even conscious that they were inspired.... The divine action respects every constituent element of the writer's make-up, and at the same time governs them so decisively that they never cease to be under the influence of the Spirit."
--Charlier, CHRISTIAN APPROACH TO THE BIBLE

9. Moslems believe that their Holy Book, the Koran, was given to Mohammed by an angel; Mormons believe that the Book of Mormons was given to Joseph Smith written in golden letters. How does their belief differ from Christian and Jewish belief about the BIBLE?

10. If you played a record by the great tenor, Enrico Caruso, you would hear not only the master's voice, but also many other sounds which are the result of the imperfections of our recording methods. How does this resemble reading the Bible?

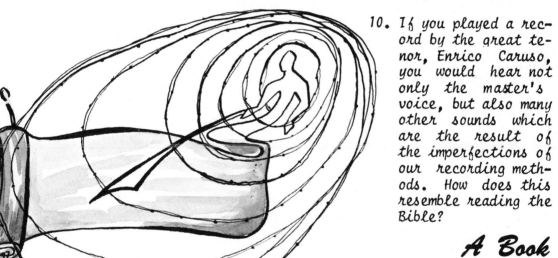

A Book of Three-Dimensions

The fact that the Bible has both a divine and at least one human author makes it richer in meaning than a merely human book. In order to understand it, therefore, you must see it in each of its three dimensions.

a. What the Bible Meant to the Human Author

- His language, culture and thought patterns were of an age far removed from us in space and time. We will understand his message only if we know his background, his purpose in writing, and the literary form he used. As we discuss each book of the Bible, we will investigate these aspects.

11. *What modern sciences have made available much of this information in recent years?*

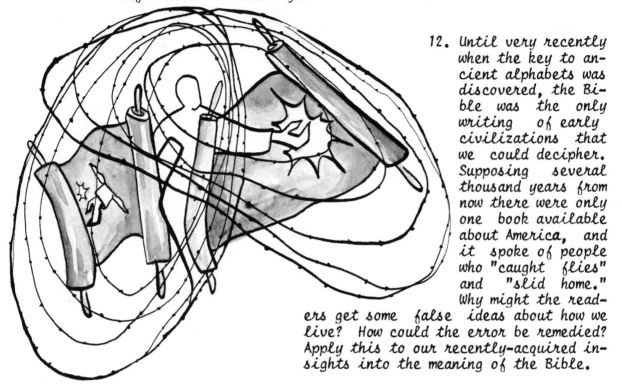

12. *Until very recently when the key to ancient alphabets was discovered, the Bible was the only writing of early civilizations that we could decipher. Supposing several thousand years from now there were only one book available about America, and it spoke of people who "caught flies" and "slid home." Why might the readers get some false ideas about how we live? How could the error be remedied? Apply this to our recently-acquired insights into the meaning of the Bible.*

If we want to grasp the author's meaning, we must keep in mind that he always wrote from the perspective of RELIGIOUS truth. With regard to HISTORY and SCIENCE, he could have the same mistaken notions that were common in his day without in any way impairing the truth of his message. The author cannot be accused of error unless he has made a deliberate judgment on the specific matter and intends to present it as true.

13. *The movie "Inherit the Wind" is based on a true incident, the famous Scopes trial, in which two famous lawyers violently disagreed about the true meaning of the Bible. Prepare one of the scenes from the book of the same name to illustrate for the class the two opposing positions.*

14. *The Bible records history, but not in the scientific style of modern historians. The biblical writer was always more interested in the MEANING behind the events than in the detailed reporting of the event. In what sense does the Civil War book, UNCLE TOM'S CABIN, contain history? What truth does the author make a judgment on, and intend to present to his readers?*

b. *What the Bible Means to the Divine Author*

- Each inspired author of the Bible conveys some fraction of God's truth, but since he does not see the whole picture, his words may have some meaning of which he is not aware, but which the Principal Author (God) intends. When we read the Old Testament in the light of Christ, the thought of the author becomes transformed in a way unforeseen except by God. God's over-all vision, because He sees revelation in reference to Christ, gives a new dimension to the limited outlook of the human author.

15. *Why is it profitable, even for those who were participating in the plays, for the football coach to show films of the game to the team?*

16. *Have you ever read a detective story backward? How would your view of the first clue differ from that of someone who had just begun to read the story?*

17. *When the biblical writer described how the Israelites put the blood of the sacrificed lamb on their door-posts at the Passover, he merely saw it as a sign by which the followers of Moses could be identified. What meaning does it have in the light of Christ's Redemption?*

THE BIBLE DOESN'T TELL US HOW THE HEAVENS GO BUT HOW TO GO TO HEAVEN

19

c. What the Bible Means to You

        - We have seen that God speaks to people not so much by the written statements of the Bible as through His creative activity in human affairs. The Bible tells us of the occasions when God has acted upon the lives of men. But we know that God's actions are eternal and unchangeable--what He has done HE IS STILL DOING. So when you read that centuries ago He called Abraham to be His friend, you come into direct contact with that eternal call to friendship that is now directed to YOU. When you read that He delivered His people from the bonds of slavery and brought them to the Promised Land, you are exposed to that gracious saving power that can deliver YOU from the shackles of fear and weakness and bring you to your own personal fulfillment. The Bible is not merely a record of past events --it is a special delivery letter with your name and address on it.

   18. *The Church alone, to whom God has committed revelation, can decide what books are inspired and what is the message these books convey. In what sense is "private" interpretation" of the Bible not only permitted, but even encouraged?*

When Amos thunders out to the people of Bethel

that they are guilty of wrongdoing....

He not only tells us

what was wrong in Bethel--

He is telling us what is wrong in

Minneapolis
or Houston
or Grovers Corners

or

wherever we may be living

today.

--Robert McAfee Brown
THE BIBLE SPEAKS TO YOU

Hello! Are You There?

In the Bible, God confronts man and says: "This is who I am! Now what is YOUR RESPONSE to this unveiling of Myself?" God is both able and willing to bring you from the Egypt of childhood into the Promised Land of Christian maturity, but your own personal history of salvation, like God's Grand Design, will develop from the interplay of two factors --God's INVITATION and your RESPONSE. When God speaks to you in the Bible, you must listen with your HEART. Then His Word will ACT in you, will make you NEW.

19. Plan a "listening experience" for the class. Read the Gospel of John, Chapter 9. Make sure that the atmosphere is conducive to listening. Allow a brief pause after the reading for a personal response. Conclude with a short prayer as the community response.

The Dialogue of the Liturgy

The liturgy of the Mass and the Sacraments offers us the most favorable occasions to meet God. In the first part of the Mass, He comes to us in His life-giving Word; in the Eucharist He invites us to a life-giving union with His Risen Body. Our response should take the same form-- by word (genuine prayer) and by action (positive acceptance of His love and surrender of selfish desires).

20. The Church has always reverenced the Bible as the book made sacred by God's Presence. What evidence do you find of this in liturgical practice?

> When we read a passage in God's Book, we must think of it,
> not as a text to be perused
> or an idea to be dissected,
>
> but as God Himself coming into our tent
> to speak to us face to face
>
> as a man speaks to his friend.
>
> --Louis Evely, THAT MAN IS YOU.

So You See...

If you want to make friends, you must take off your mask, stop playing the role. You must speak and live from the depth of your being and address yourself to the other person in the depth of his being. Going out to others will help you to go out to God, and in meeting God and others you will find your true self.

> Man is made to be "I" and say "Thou"--
> That is what the Bible tells us.

It's Your Move!

1. Why is it so important for your development as a person to have friends?

2. Explain the characteristics of self-revelation.

3. How does God use historical events and persons to reveal Himself?

4. What is the role of the People of God in His plan?

5. Show how the Bible came to be.

6. Why are both God and man considered true authors of the Bible?

7. Show by example why it is important to know an author's background, his purpose, and the literary form he is using in order to understand correctly what he writes.

8. In what sense is the Bible free from error?

9. Show how the words of the human author may have a deeper meaning than he realizes.

10. When you read the Bible, you are not a spectator of what is presented there but a participant in the drama. How can this be, since the incidents occurred so long ago?

11. With what dispositions should we read the Bible?

12. Show how the liturgy involves both God and us in work and action.

13. Give three basic guidelines that will help you to make friends.

Further Insights

Know...

Prepare a report for the class on the topic assigned to you from this list:

The Canon of Sacred Scriptures
The contribution of modern science to biblical knowledge
The various translations of the Bible
The Bible used by both Protestants and Catholics
President Kennedy's use of the Bible
The science of exegesis
The contribution of archaeology to biblical studies
The Bible and the Dead Sea Scrolls
The use of the Bible in civil functions; e.g., court,
    presidential oath
The influence of the Bible on Thomas Jefferson's thought
The Bible in literature
The Bible in music
The Bible in art
The Bible in the Mass

...And Love the Bible

1. Compose a brief prayer to be said before reading the Bible.
2. Mark the passages in your Bible that have a personal appeal for you.
3. If you do not have a family Bible, purchase one.
4. Try to share your knowledge and love of the Bible by discussing what you have learned with your family. You might introduce the custom of family Bible reading.
5. Design a Back-to-the-Bible campaign poster.

Bible Devotion

PRELIMINARY COMMENT: It is in historical events that God has spoken to us and it is the Bible that transmits to us the account of these events. And so the Bible is read in our assemblies. . .Jesus, in the midst of the assembly, speaks to us when the Holy Book is opened. As He did once before at Nazareth, He says to us: "This day the Gospel is proclaimed to you, and the promise is fulfilled and realized." ...But it is more than just a matter of reading. We have to listen and respond. Through Christ we have a dialogue with the Father.

--Rev. Robert W. Case, O.S.B., LIVING LIGHT, Summer, 1964

On the Word of God

ENTRANCE HYMN (as the Bible is carried to the lectern prepared for it and placed on it open and facing the class. The lectern may be draped with a liturgically colored cloth.) Come Holy Ghost.

LEADER: O God, hear our prayer.
CLASS: And let our cry come unto you.

LEADER: For the presence of Christ living and acting in the midst of our assembly that we may attend to the Word: O God hear our prayer.
CLASS: And let our cry come unto you.

LEADER: For the presence of Christ living and acting in the midst of our assembly that we may respond to the Word: O God hear our prayer.
CLASS: And let our cry come unto you.

FIRST READER: A blessing, pray, that I may worthily proclaim the word of God.
LEADER: May the Lord Christ be in your heart and on your lips so that all here present may hear the Word and respond to it.
ALL: Amen.

FIRST READER: (Bows to enthroned Bible, turns to face class and announces:) A reading from the Book of Exodus (3:1-14)
ALL: Glory to you, O Lord.

   READING

FIRST READER: (Comments on reading) Our God is not a God without a face or a name, a far-off divinity before whom we fall in fear. Our God is a God who speaks. He is concerned about us and He wants to help us. He reveals Himself to us and as we listen to His Word we are brought into direct contact with His gracious concern which today is directed toward each one of us, just as it was directed toward Moses and His people of old.

LEADER: Let us pray. . . (all pray silently for several moments)

LEADER: (Response, Psalm 4) Many say, "Oh, that we might see better times!"
ALL: O Lord, let the light of your countenance shine upon us!

LEADER: You put gladness into my heart, more than when grain and wine abound.
ALL: O Lord, let the light of your countenance shine upon us!

LEADER: As soon as I lie down, I fall peacefully asleep, for you alone, O Lord, bring security to my dwelling.
ALL: O Lord, let the light of your countenance shine upon us!

SECOND READER: A blessing, pray, that I may worthily proclaim the Word of God.
LEADER: May the Lord Christ be in your heart and on your lips so that all here present may hear the Word and respond to it.
ALL: Amen.

SECOND READER: (Bows to enthroned Bible, turns to face class and announces:) A reading from the Second Letter to Timothy (3:14-17).
ALL: Glory to you, O Lord.

    READING

SECOND READER: (Comments on reading) God's revelation of Himself which comes to us in Sacred Scripture has the power to change us. In this encounter with God's Word we meet Jesus Christ, the Word made flesh. If we open ourselves in faith to His action in this meeting, He will call forth in us all the hidden good that only love can see and bring to light.

LEADER: Let us pray. . . (All pray silently for several moments)

LEADER: (Response, Psalm 33) I sought the Lord, and he answered me and delivered me from all my fears.
ALL: Taste and see how good the Lord is.

LEADER: Look to him that you may be radiant with joy, and your faces may not blush with shame.
ALL: Taste and see how good the Lord is.

LEADER: When the afflicted man called out, the Lord heard, and from all his distress he saved him.
ALL: Taste and see how good the Lord is.

THIRD READER: A blessing, pray, that I may worthily proclaim the Word of God.
LEADER: May the Lord Christ be in your heart and on your lips so that all here present may hear the Word and respond to it.
ALL: Amen.

THIRD READER: (Bows to enthroned Bible, turns to face class and announces:) Please stand for a reading from the Gospel of Luke (8:4-15).
ALL: Glory to you, O Lord.

READING

THIRD READER: (Comments on reading) The Word of God will be fruitful to the degree that our hearts are open to receive it. Our growth as a person is a gradual process determined by the interplay of what we are by God's grace and what choices we make in our day-to-day affairs. We will become our best selves when we cooperate with the Sower by providing fertile ground for His seed.

LEADER: Let us pray. . . (All pray silently for several moments)

LEADER: (Response, Psalm 64) You have visited the land and watered it; greatly have you enriched it. God's watercourses are filled; you have prepared the grain.
ALL: You have crowned the year with your bounty, and your paths overflow with a rich harvest.

LEADER: Thus have you prepared the land: drenching its furrows, breaking up its clods, softening it with showers, blessing its yield.
ALL: You have crowned the year with your bounty, and your paths overflow with a rich harvest.

LEADER: The fields are garmented with flocks and the valleys blanketed with grain. They shout and sing for joy.
ALL: You have crowned the year with your bounty, and your paths overflow with a rich harvest.

(If a priest is available, the students' bibles could be blessed and then venerated by kissing the open gospel page. If the number is small, one at a time could bow to the enthroned Bible.)

LEADER: (Holding large Bible high) May the blessing of the Almighty Holy One, Father, Son, and Holy Spirit, descend upon you and remain with you now and always and unto endless ages of ages.
ALL: Amen.

RECESSIONAL HYMN: Now Thank We All Our God

Chapter 3 - God's Free Choice

A Freshman Once Said

Does God really care about me?

"Oh, I know God loves us, but does He love ME, John (or Judy) Simpson? It doesn't seem as if He could, and besides why should He? If He sees through my disguises, I'm really not **very** lovable. When you come right down to it, why should He love any man? When you love someone, it's almost as if you needed him in order to be happy. I'm sure God doesn't need ME! I'm not necessary to His happiness!"

1. Can you always give a reason for liking people?

2. Discuss the motives behind these choices: a couple chooses a child for adoption; a sales clerk marries the president of the company ; a man is selected as an ambassador.

3. Can you be friends with someone who doesn't want to be friends with you?

4. If your friend asked you to do something that seemed ridiculous and said he couldn't explain why it was necessary to do it, would you do it for him?

Light from the Old Testament

A New Beginning

Anthropologists tell us that men have been on this earth for at least 1,750,000 years. History covers only the last 5,000 of those years, less than one per cent of the time.

The first historical record we have of any direct communication between God and man dates back to about 1850 B. C. At that time in the Fertile Crescent (comprising Egypt, Palestine, Syria, the Tigris-Euphrates Valley to the Persian Gulf) lived the herdsman sheik, Thare, and his clan. Under pressure of invaders they moved from Ur in southern Mesopotamia to Haran in the North. One of Thare's sons was Abram, who, like his father, worshipped the pagan gods of their people, especially the Moon-goddess, the patron deity of their city. God revealed Himself to this man, reopening his dialogue with mankind by a personal intervention in history.

> 5. Draw a time-line showing man's existence on earth. Include the time of Abram, the birth of Christ, and today's date.

God Seeks a Friend
Genesis 12:1-8

God "spoke" to Abram; by some kind of religious experience, God revealed Himself to this Semitic nomad. This was enough to change his whole life.

God promised Abram: a. that his descendants would form a great people; b. that they would have a land of their own and become prosperous; and c. that the whole world would share in their blessings. The fulfillment of the promise depended on Abram's leaving his country, his kinsfolk, and above all, the native gods. The promises were very vague and general, so Abram had to have faith in God and trust that God would keep His word. It took great courage "to go forth" as the Lord commanded, risking his future on the unknown. Abram could rely on no one except God.

To be God's friend is an undeserved privilege; no one can earn it. God must take the first step. When God chooses someone, He does so out of love, not because that person is more worthy than others. Sometimes He chooses a person for the sake of what he will do for others.

> 6. How was God's choice of Abram connected with some work God wanted him to do?

> 7. Give other examples of God's calling individuals to close friendship with Him for the sake of what they would do for His people. (Hints: Luke 1:26-38; Acts 9:1-9)

Abram Says "Yes" to God

Abram believed that God would keep His promise to him because He accepted God as a trustworthy Person. He showed that he believed God by leaving the protection of his tribe and moving away to a strange land. This was quite a gamble, because as yet Abram had no proof that God would keep His promise, except God's word for it--and the odds were against his having a child in his old age.

> 8. Write a dramatic skit of the scene when Abram announces to the tribe that he is going away. Remember that he has never seen this God on whose word he is staking so much.

When Abram believed the Lord, their friendship was established. Faith is a bond that unites us to God.

> 9. What does the Bible say was the result of Abram's faith? Does being holy make you a friend of God, or does being a friend of God make you holy?

The Pact of Friendship   Genesis 15:7-20

God gave Abram a visible sign of their pact of friendship by going through a ceremony that men of that day used to seal an agreement. They would cut animals in half and walk between the pieces as if to say: "If I break this agreement, let what has happened to these animals happen to me."

> 10. Why did God give Abram this visible sign?
>
> 11. Under what form did God pass between the animals? Why is this an appropriate way for God to show His presence?
>
> 12. Why didn't Abram walk through the cut animals?
>
> 13. How do people sign a covenant today?

Because God's promise was not only for Abram but for all his descendants, his name was changed to Abraham--father of a multitude--to show that he had a new position.

14. *Give examples of other names being changed to show a new position.*

Those of Abraham's descendants who believed in God and His promise were circumcised as a sign of their faith. At that time circumcision was part of the rite by which a boy was initiated into manhood. It was made into a religious ceremony by which a person showed that he believed in the God who had revealed Himself to Abraham.

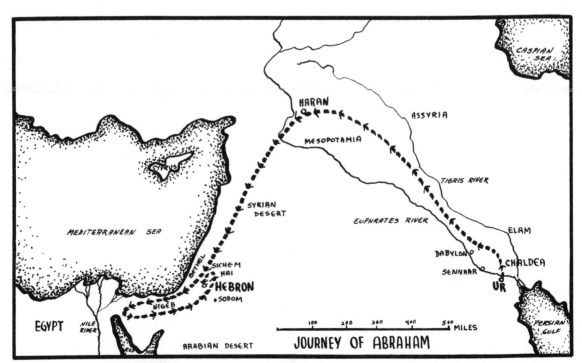

JOURNEY OF ABRAHAM

15. *Find evidence that the practice of giving a name and of circumcizing boys was still going on at the time of Christ.*

The Test of Friendship

Genesis 21:1-8
22:1-19

God finally gave Abraham and Sara a son, whom they called Isaac ("tizqah" - to laugh). He was the first installment on the fulfillment of God's promise. Abraham was delighted and his faith in God grew stronger.

But as Isaac got older, Abraham began to worry when he saw his Chanaanite neighbors offer their first sons to their gods. Perhaps his God also wanted him to offer Isaac in sacrifice! He was really in a predicament. If he refused to sacrifice Isaac, he would break his friendship with God; if he killed his son, it would be impossible for God's promise to come true. Fortunately, God revealed to him that He was not like the Chanaanite gods--He was not pleased with human sacrifice.

16. Show how the following words from Genesis 22 are related to the story of redemption:

> only son
> beloved son
> mountain
> wood for sacrifice
> Isaac to carry
> walk together
> the lamb for a victim
> bound his son

17. Why did the fate of humanity hang in the balance at the moment of Abraham's decision? Can you think of another moment when, so to speak, creation "held its breath" waiting for an answer?

Light from the New Testament

Christ Seeks a Friend

God's call to friendship begun in Abraham continued down through the ages until He spoke in a human voice through His Son Jesus Christ.

18. *Luke 5:1-11 - To what did Jesus call the four fishermen? What sign did He give them of His trustworthiness? How was their response like Abraham's?*

19. *Luke 5:27-32 - To what did Jesus call Levi? How was his response like Abraham's? Did Christ call Levi because he was holy?*

20. *John 15:12-17 - Who took the first step in their friendship with Christ? In whose name was he offering friendship? What were the conditions of the friendship?*

Jesus Makes a Pact of Friendship

21. *John 13:1-11 - What proof do you have that Christ's friendship is not a "sometime thing"? What was the visible sign of their friendship.*

A Friend Indeed

22. *John 6:48-72 - How was the disciples' faith in Jesus tested? In what way was their test like Abraham's? How was Peter's response like Abraham's?*

23. *Mark 14:43-52 - What did you learn in this passage about friendship with Christ?*

It is God's very nature to GIVE. He is the Father because He gives Himself to the Son. When the Father calls us, it is because He has a need of giving Himself to us, of entering into a relation with us. The truth is that God loves us, not because we are so good, but because HE is good. God's love for us is His NEED to give Himself to us.

24. *Discuss:* *Some people say, "I love you because I need you";*
God says, "I need you because I love you."

From the beginning, God has been calling ALL men. He wants to be Father to every man. His call comes to us especially through His Son Jesus. It is in the Only-begotten Son that we, too, become sons.

25. *How do you know that God is calling you to be His friend? Ask a Sister, a Brother, or a priest to tell you how she or he recognized God's call. The inspired writer merely says: "The Lord said to Abram." But remember that the Lord speaks through signs, both within you and outside you. What might some of those signs be?*

Make That Connection!

A LIVING God calls every man into a loving relation with Himself. When you call your friend on the telephone, there is no connection between you until you answer. So when God calls you, there is no relation with Him until you answer Him. If you let the phone ring, when you know who is calling, you show that you do not want to be connected with your friend. Faith is answering God's call to friendship by saying, "Yes, I want to be connected with You."

26. *What does it mean to have faith in people?*
in a doctor?
a teacher?
a friend?

Faith Is a Journey

If by faith, we decide to "throw·in our lot with God," to accept Him and everything He stands for, it will mean for us, as it did for Abraham, rearranging our lives, not just once but again and again.

27. Compare your decision of faith to the astronauts' venture into space. Consider the various stages.

TAKE-OFF	IN-BETWEEN STAGE	DESTINATION
1. Familiar things	1. Uncertainty	1. Wonderful new sights
2. People I love	2. Inconveniences	2. Sense of fulfillment
3. Security	3. Hardships	3. Difficulties forgotten
4. Certainty	4. Feeling of strangeness	

28. Tell about some people whose reply to God's demand meant an entirely new kind of life for them.

29. How would the possession of a strong Christian faith affect your attitude toward:

        a. prayer?
        b. material things?
        c. personal limitations, such as lack of talent, personality, success, etc.?
        d. other people?
        e. the missions?
        f. death?

Faith Is a Risk

When we commit ourselves to God in faith we are, in a sense, putting our lives in His hands. Being God, He may sometimes ask us to do things which we cannot understand. Sometimes there will be no convincing evidence for what He says, merely His word. Faith means moving out into the unknown, oftentimes sure of only one thing--that God is with you.

30. What is the difference between doubting God and not understanding the things He says?

31. There are two ways of strengthening your faith: 1. By studying the truths of faith; 2. By deepening your relationship with Christ through prayer and the sacraments. Discuss their relative values.

Faith Is Hoping Against Hope

Because God's plan and His promises are so much greater than we are, faith will present difficulties. These difficulties can be the occasion by which we attach ourselves more firmly to God because we realize that His power makes possible what is humanly impossible.

32. God promised much greater things to Abraham than he ever realized. Show how Abraham's understanding of God's promises differed from our understanding of what is meant by: 1. a people, 2. a land, 3. world influence. In what ways is our understanding still vague?

We Answer in Christ

Faith is first of all accepting, not a body of doctrine, but God as a Person who loves you and wants to do great things for you. It is your answer to God's call to friendship. It means that you accept not only God, but all the things He stands for. What God stands for is most clearly expressed in Christ. It is in Him that God calls us and in Him that we answer God. Without Christ, we could not have known God's love for us; without Him, we could not have loved God as a son.

Call of God ←——————— CHRIST ———————→ Response of man

It is because Christ your Brother responded so perfectly to His Father's call that you can respond to yours.

33. Learn John 14:6 by memory. Be able to explain what it means.

Sign of Faith

Judaism was a call to faith in God's promise; circumcision was the visible sign that a man believed in that promise. Christianity is a call to life and love in Christ, the fulfillment of God's promise, and baptism is the visible sign of Faith in Christ.

34. Did you have faith when you were baptized? Your baptism then was a sign of whose faith? When will it become a sign of your faith?

35. Examine the liturgy of baptism for evidence that it is a sign of faith.

Abraham is the Father of all believers. In his response to God's Word, we read our own vocation to faith.

36. In what ways does our faith resemble Abraham's?

37. There are several references to Abraham in the liturgy. Consult the Canon of the Mass, the burial service, and the blessing of a house, and explain why the Church refers to Abraham in these prayers.

It's Your Move!

1. Why did God choose Abraham in preference to one of his neighbors?

2. What called forth Abraham's faith in God?

3. How does the story of Isaac remind you of the story of our redemption?

4. How does God's love for us differ from the way we love others?

5. What difficulties did Abraham's faith in God have to overcome? How did these difficulties affect his faith?

6. Why is faith a risk?

7. Show how God's promises to Abraham were fulfilled in a way Abraham never dreamed of.

8. Why is Christ our way to faith?

9. Describe the baptismal ceremony as the sign of faith.

10. Show how Abraham is the Father of all believers.

11. Why must God's love for you be a very personal love?

Reflection

Evely points out that our faith in God's word is measured by our faith in His love, that we don't really believe He speaks to us because we don't really believe He loves us. Or if we do, we don't believe He loves us individually. You cannot have a personal relationship with a crowd. God's love is very much a personal relationship, a special love and understanding for the unique individual that is YOU!

Further Insights

The Jews were proud of their ancestor, Abraham, and they preserved many stories about him.

Genesis 13 - Abraham shows great generosity. Locate the places referred to on the map.

Genesis 16 and 21:9-21 - Sarah's invitation to her husband to have children by her maid-servant shows the great importance the Israelites attached to having a family, especially a boy to be the heir. However, the situation that resulted caused jealousy. St. Paul uses this incident to compare the Old and New Testament. (Gal. 4)

Genesis 18 and 19:23-29 - Hospitality was an important tradition at this time. Abraham entertained three strangers who were heavenly visitors in disguise. The bargaining scene shows Abraham's intimacy with God.

Look up these topics and make a report to the class:

    The heroic faith of Joan of Arc
    Dr. Tom Dooley, a modern Abraham
    St. Paul's list of "giants of faith" in Hebrews, 11
    The World of Abraham's Ancestors (2000 B.C.)
    America's Destiny - from President Kennedy's Inaugural
            Address
    Charlie Brown's faith in Lucy

Chapter 4 - Man and God's Providence

A Freshman Once Said
Is God's plan a straight-jacket?

"You know, this bit about a 'plan'--I don't like it. It makes me feel like a puppet. Everything's worked out ahead of time so what I do doesn't really matter. If it's God's plan, I'm sure it's a good one, but----well, it's something like an assembly program. If the teacher has a good idea and has it all worked out and we just put it on, it will probably be a good program. But not nearly as good as when the teacher has a good idea and we all work it out together. Even if it isn't exactly perfect, it has more life or something, that way. I was just wondering how does God's plan work?"

1. Discuss the relative merits of being given a program already worked out and of working one out together with the teacher.

2. What are some conditions that would influence your evaluation?

Light from the Old Testament

Abraham passed on the torch of faith in God's promises to his son Isaac. Little is said of Isaac except that he married Rebecca and had twin sons, Esau and Jacob. These sons, so opposite in character and appearance, were the founders of two peoples who were always hostile to each other, the Edomites and the Israelites. These stories were passed down orally for generations before they were written. Although basically true, they are "slanted" by the biblical writer to emphasize the message he wanted to get across: GOD WAS WORKING FOR HIS PEOPLE IN ALL THE EVENTS OF THEIR HISTORY.

Forcing God's Hand

Genesis 27:1-28:5

Rebecca, convinced that Jacob was better suited to take over the leadership of the family than was Esau, did not hesitate to use dishonest means to bring this about.

3. Drawing your material from the biblical account (you might also want to consult Genesis 25:21-34), write a character description of Jacob and Esau and decide whether or not you agree with Rebecca's preference.

4. God certainly wanted the revelation He had made to Abraham to continue in his family. Do you think He approved of Rebecca and Jacob's deception? Was this part of His plan?

5. The plot was successful, but it caused many people to suffer. How did the various people involved have to suffer as a result of it?

Jacob Wins a Fortune and a Family

Genesis 29:1-31
30:22-24
31:1-42

Jacob had to leave home because of the tension that resulted from his having outwitted his brother, but God was with him and many good things happened to him in his new life.

6. The biblical writers often speak as if God were directly responsible for all the things that happen. Find examples of this in these passages.

7. Show how God is only partly responsible if the sun is shining into this room.

8. Who is responsible for Jacob's acquiring a large herd, God or Jacob?

9. If your mother tells you not to eat any more of the candy that is on the table so that your face won't break out, but she just stands there and watches you eat it, is she responsible for your "blooming" face?

41

10. *Who is responsible for Laban's cheating Jacob?*

11. *What things in your life are determined by God? What things do you determine?*

Jacob Wins a Match and a Destiny Genesis 32:22-33

Jacob was pledged to faith in his grandfather's God when he was circumcized, but it was important that he encounter God more directly. The sacred writer depicts his struggle to come to a personal faith as a wrestling match with an angel. When he had successfully passed through this crisis in his life, he was given a new name "Israel," which means "one who prevails with God," that is, a favorite of God.

This name came to be applied also to all of Jacob's descendants; they were known as Israel, God's beloved people.

The name "Israel" may come from a Hebrew verb meaning "to persevere" or from another verb meaning "to rule as a prince." The action refers, of course, to Jacob's wrestling with the messenger of God.

The name and history of Jacob-Israel became a prized heritage and a sign of God's promise even for the early members of the Church. Paul, the Jew who persecuted the Christians , could say to the people in the synagogue at Antioch:

> "Israelites and you who fear God, hearken.
> The God of the people of Israel
> chose our fathers
> and exalted the people
> when they were sojourners in the land of Egypt,
> and with uplifted arm
> led them first out of it...."
>
> He raised up David to be their king,
> and to him he bore witness
> and said,
> 'I have found David,
> the son of Jesse,
> a man after my heart,
> who will do all that I desire.'
>
> From his offspring,
> God
> according to promise
> brought to Israel a Savior,
> Jesus." (Acts 13:16-17, 22-23)

Israel, the people who "struggled with God," is at once the people favored by God. Israel is God's People. Israel, its Savior come, is a figure of the Church.

12. Read these beautiful passages in the book of Isaiah, 43:1-4 and 44:1-5, for examples of how sometimes God addresses one man as if he were a whole nation and at other times speaks to an entire people as if they were one person.

13. Make a chart showing Jacob's family tree, beginning with Abraham and including Jacob's twelve sons. Cf. Genesis 35:23-26.

Joseph Loses...and Wins

Genesis 37, 39:1 - 46:7

Jacob had a favorite, too; it was Joseph, the son of his beloved Rachel. Joseph is often the victim of injustice. In spite of this, he remains faithful to God and lives to see all this evil turn to good, not only for himself, but for his whole family and for the furthering of God's plan of salvation.

14. Sometimes the sacred writer uses two slightly different traditions in his account, although they don't agree perfectly. Compare the two explanations of how to dispose of Joseph: one by Judah and another by Ruben. Can you find other examples of the two traditions?

15. Archeologists testify to the accuracy of the information in Genesis on Egyptian background and customs. Prepare a report for the class on Egyptian history and culture during this period (1700-1200 B.C.) highlighting the details that are related to the Scripture passage; e.g., magic, dreams, agriculture, herding.

16. Take an incident in Joseph's life in which he was forced to make a decision. Try to imagine the outcome if he had acted differently than he did and rewrite the story from that angle.

17. Dramatize your favorite scene from the story of Joseph.

18. Of all Jacob's sons, Joseph seems the one most fitted to be the ancestor of the Savior. Read 49:8-10 to find which brother was so honored.

Light from the New Testament

When you begin to wonder whether God's plan is so iron-clad that there's no room for you in it, read the accounts of these two men: their call to a role in God's plan, their act of treason, and the outcome.

PETER   Mark 14:32-40   Mark 14:66-72   John 21:15-17

JUDAS   Matthew 26:47-50   Matthew 27:3-5   Acts 1:15-22

19. Were both of these men part of God's plan? In what sense did God's plan change? Both men sinned gravely against their Lord. What good was God able to bring from Peter's sin?

But the foolish things of the world has God chosen to put to shame the 'wise,' and the weak things of the world has God chosen to put to shame the strong; and the base things of the world and the despised has God chosen, and the things that are not, to bring to naught the things that are; lest any flesh should pride itself before Him.
      1 Cor. 1:27-29

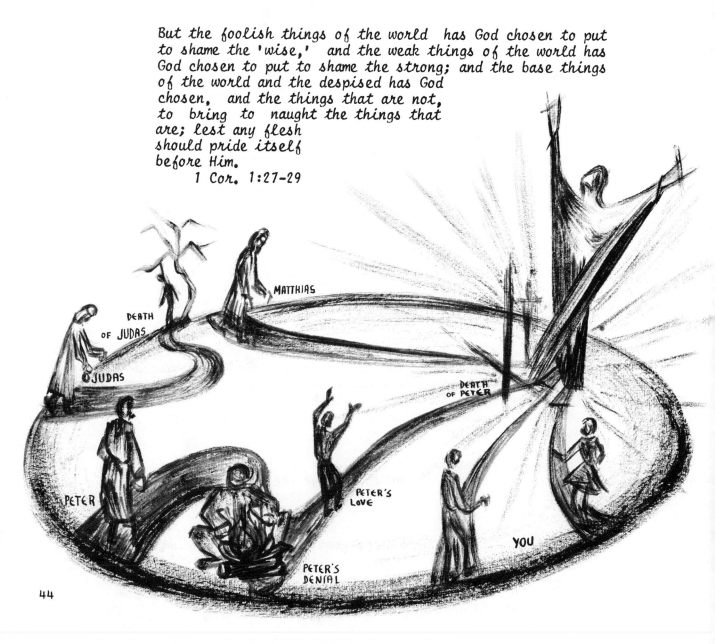

DEATH OF JUDAS

MATTHIAS

JUDAS

DEATH OF PETER

PETER

PETER'S LOVE

YOU

PETER'S DENIAL

44

So You See...

Although God has a plan and will certainly see that it is achieved, the carrying out of His plan is a cooperative venture. The plan is flexible enough to allow us to make real decisions within it. He gives us the raw materials--an orderly world that acts according to laws, a mind to think things out with, various personal talents--and the design, and tells us to go to work. He is always concerned and responds to our call for help, but He respects us too much to take the brush out of our hands. And even when we blunder, great artist that He is, He can rework that part of the pattern so that it not only covers up the mistake we made, but makes the design more beautiful than ever.

20. Using the comparison of a composer of orchestral music and a player who is making mistakes, express the idea that is contained in the figure of the painter.

21. In the Easter Vigil, there is a beautiful phrase, "O felix culpa!" which means "O happy sin of Adam and Eve!" How could such a tragedy be called "happy"?

22. St. Paul in his Letter to the Romans (8:28) says that for those who love God all things work together unto good, and St. Augustine adds, "Even sin!" How can your sins "work together unto good"?

A BIT OF ADVICE WHEN YOU HAVE A PROBLEM:

WORK as if everything depended on YOU
PRAY as if everything depended on GOD

The Ladder of the Liturgy

Genesis 28:10-22

The vision Jacob had of the ladder with the angels of God going up and down on it reminds us of the liturgy where the two-way traffic between God and man takes place. Christ carries on this two-way commerce with God and in Him our worship goes to the Father and divine life comes to us.

23. To mark the places sanctified by God's presence, men set up a stone and anointed it with oil. Sometimes they would re-visit these "sanctuaries" where they had met God. Of what does this remind you in the Catholic Church?

24. If you were choosing some phrases from this passage for the Mass of the Dedication of a Church, which ones would you choose and why?

25. What line contains an appropriate prayer for the end of Mass?

It's Your Move!

1. Are the accounts of the patriarchs in Genesis stories or history?

2. What is the religious message that the author wants to convey in these passages?

3. What was the result when Rebecca took God's plan into her own hands?

4. When an apple falls from a tree, the biblical writer would say, "God plucked the apple." What does he mean by the expression?

5. How are we to understand the expressions of the biblical writer such as "God took away your father's stock and gave it to me"?

6. What is the meaning of the word "Israel" and to whom does it refer?

7. Apply the proverb "God writes straight with crooked lines" to the story of Joseph.

8. What do the lives of Peter and Judas tell us about God's plan?

9. Show how God's plan is a cooperative venture.

10. How is Jacob's ladder like the liturgy?

11. What effect does it have on you to know that the details of the plan are still being worked out?

Reflection

When someone has treated you very unjustly, could you say with Joseph: "Do not fear; can I take the place of God? You intended evil against me, but God intended it for good, to do as he has done today, namely, to save the lives of many people. Therefore, do not fear." (Genesis 50:19-21)

Further Insights

The Dying Patriarch - Genesis 49

This poetry was composed long after the death of Jacob; it is probably an ancient tradition touched up by a writer. The three older brothers are passed over and Judah is given the rights of the firstborn. Jacob had adopted Joseph's two sons, Ephraim and Manasse in Ruben's place, so that Joseph would get a double share of the inheritance. In the original Hebrew, the descriptions contain much play on words that cannot be translated. Why does St. John (Apoc. 5:5) call Our Lord the lion of Judah?

The Talking Ass - Numbers 22 - 24

This is one of the most fascinating stories of the Bible. It is a folk tale adapted from the literature of the Near East to bring out the fact that God can disrupt the carefully laid plans of the enemies of His people and change their curses to blessings. "He can use even an ass to bring His word to those who think they know everything." (Tos) There is a similar situation in John 9:24-34. Have you ever experienced this truth in your own life?

At that time, Jesus spoke and said "I praise thee Father, Lord of heaven and earth, that thou didst hide these things from the wise and prudent, and didst reveal them to little ones. Yes, Father, for such was thy good pleasure. Matt. 11:25-26

Chapter 5 -
Our Covenant Obligation

A Freshman Once Said
Who wants to be holy?

"Me holy? Definitely not--and I'm not sure that I want to be. I'm not the 'halo' type, and besides, it takes all the fun out of life. Now don't get me wrong, I'm a reasonably decent kid--I keep out of serious trouble. But this holiness bit, I just don't buy it. It doesn't make sense to me; unless, of course, as you say, maybe I don't know what it's all about."

1. What is the difference between being a "good" person and being a "religious" person? Do they always go together?

2. Why should we do good and avoid evil?

3. What makes some things good and other things evil?

Light from the Old Testament

The Jews consider the Book of Exodus as the most important book of the Bible because it records the beginning of their history as the People of God. Exodus revolves around a MAN and an EVENT. The man is Moses, the inspired leader of the Chosen People, and the event is God's marvelous intervention in their behalf to bring them out of slavery in Egypt and to make them His people.

This book is a religious epic woven together by various inspired editors over a long period of time from the four streams of literary traditions that grew up in the Hebrew community. The events are told in a very dramatic style to emphasize the wonder of God's saving power.

I Have Seen Your Misery

Exodus 3 and 4

The descendants of Abraham had fallen on hard times in Egypt. In the 400 years since Joseph's death, new rulers had come into power and they had forced the Hebrews living there into a kind of slave labor.

By a special act of God, Moses grew up in Pharaoh's court and was well educated. When his divided loyalties made trouble, he fled into the Arabian desert and became a shepherd. Here he meets God and is commissioned to lead his people to freedom.

4. *Moses is reluctant to assume this responsibility. He had a healthy distrust of his own unaided ability. What objections does he raise and how does God answer them?*

Your name tells WHO you are, distinguishes you from everyone else. God told Moses that His name is YAHWEH, which means "the One who is always there for you." ("Jehovah" is an incorrect spelling of the word.) By revealing His name, God expressed His nature, His power and fidelity and His desire to be on intimate terms with His people. In later Judaism, the Name came to be too sacred to pronounce and the title "Lord" (Adonai) was used instead.

5. *What is expressed by the name of "Jesus"?*

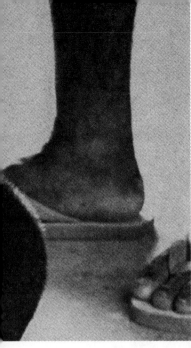

Let My People Go!

The sacred writer builds up suspense in this great conflict between Yahweh and the Pharaoh. This causes Egypt to become in biblical history the symbol of the temporal power that tries to frustrate God's plan. Although the plagues

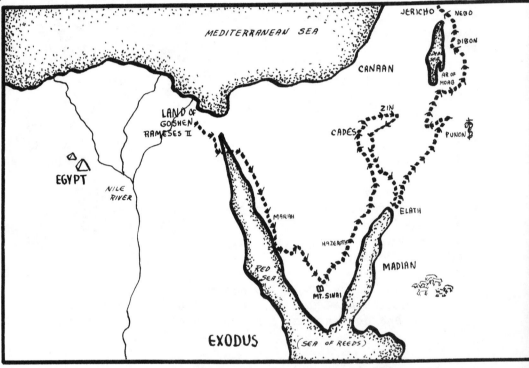

MEDITERRANEAN SEA

JERICHO NEBO
DIBON
CANAAN
AR OF MOAB
LAND OF GOSHEN
RAMESES II
ZIN
CADES
PUNON
EGYPT
NILE RIVER
MARAH
ELATH
HAZEROTH
RED SEA
MADIAN
MT. SINAI
EXODUS
(SEA OF REEDS)

were mostly natural phenomena, they were for the Jews clear indications of God's power working through nature in their behalf. They convinced everyone except the Pharaoh.

6. *For those who have faith, God's activity in the very ordinary events of everyday life is quite apparent. Have you ever recognized God's hand in your life?*

7. *Phyllis McGinley, in the first eight lines of her poem "Conversation in Avila," captures perfectly the flavor of a charming anecdote about St. Teresa of Avila:*

50

Teresa was God's familiar. She often spoke
To Him informally,
As if together they shared some heavenly joke.
Once, watching stormily
Her heart's ambitions wither to odds and ends,
With all to start anew,
She cried, "If this is the way You treat Your friends,
No wonder You have so few."
　　　　　　　　--from TIMES THREE

Compare her thought with Moses' speech in Exodus 5:22-23.

8. Dramatize the scene in Pharaoh's Court from Marc Connelly's GREEN PASTURES, Part II, Scene 3.

9. Negro spirituals express very aptly the spirit of the biblical account. Sing "Go Down, Moses" trying to get the feel of the situation.

1. When Israel was in Egypt Land
   Let my people go!
   Oppressed so hard they could not stand,
   Let my people go!

   CHORUS: Go down, Moses, way down in Egypt Land
   　　　　　Tell Ole Pharaoh: "Let my people go."

2. When Israel out of Egypt came,
   Let my people go!
   They left that proud oppressor's land,
   Let my people go! (CHORUS)

3. It was a dark and stormy night,
   Let my people go!
   When Moses led the Israelites,
   Oh, let my people go! (CHORUS)

4. 'Twas good ole Moses and Aaron, too,
   Let my people go!
   'Twas they that led the armies through
   Let my people go! (CHORUS)

I Will Deliver You

Exodus 12:1-42
13:17 - 14:31

It would take the tenth plague, the death of all the first-born of Egypt, to finally convince the Pharaoh that Yahweh would not take "No" for an answer. During the night when Yahweh struck, the Israelites were directed to carry out the ritual of the paschal supper and the ceremony of smearing blood on the doorposts. They never forgot that night when God adopted them as His own, and today the Passover still remains the greatest of all Jewish feasts, the symbolic acting out of their marvelous deliverance from slavery.

10. Ask a Jewish friend about their celebration of the Passover. Compare it with the scriptural account. Can you give an explanation of what the Passover means to you as a Christian?

The Hebrew term "Red Sea" really means "Reed Sea," a marshy area near lakes. Exactly how the Israelites escaped is not certain, but the combination of events that surrounded their departure was so unusual that they could not doubt that God had intervened. His saving presence among them is described as a luminous cloud visible both by day and by night.

11. The film "Exodus," adapted from the book of the same name, recounts another return of God's people to the Promised Land that took place in our century. Listen to the recording of the theme from the film and decide whether it conveys the spirit of the original Exodus.

12. Can you name some other dramatic escapes to freedom similar to the Jewish Exodus that have taken place in our day? How are they different from it?

I Shall Be Your God

Exodus 19:1-20:21

To release the Hebrew people from bondage was just the beginning. God wanted to form a partnership with them and He led them into the desert where, amid an impressive display of power, He made His proposal. If they accepted His proposition, all the power that had terrified them so would be directed against their enemies. He would provide for them and protect them always as He had in the past. But there was one condition He would insist on: they must accept the same standards of good and evil that He accepted. He loved justice and honesty and order; and, if they wanted to be associated with Him, they must love them also. These were the terms of the COVENANT He would make with them.

Speak to the whole Israelite community
and tell them: Be holy, for I, the
Lord, your God, am holy.--Lev. 19:2

13. What do you think of the terms of the agreement?

14. Why does God forbid the Israelites to make any images of Him? Why are we permitted to have images in our churches? Does a synagogue contain religious images? A moslem mosque?

15. Scripture described God as a "jealous" God. In what sense is He jealous?

52

17. Are the acts forbidden by the Commandments wrong because God forbade them, or did God forbid them because they are wrong? Would they have bad effects in our lives, even if they were not forbidden? Give an example.

You Shall Be My People

Exodus 24:3-18
Deuteronomy 26:16-19

After reading the Book of Covenant to the assembled people, Moses seals the covenant according to an ancient custom by sprinkling blood on the altar (presence of God) and on the people. The alliance is celebrated by sharing a sacrificial meal.

18. To be sprinkled with blood is not an appealing ceremony to us, but for the Israelites for whom blood was a symbol of life, it had a profound meaning. What did the ceremony express?

19. What are some signs by which we seal agreements today?

20. Read Hebrews 9:1-4 for a description of the Ark of the Covenant, a chest containing the symbols of the covenant, which was the sign of God's presence among His people. How were the manna, the rod of Aaron, and the tablets of stone related to the covenant?

21. How does our use of the word "tabernacle" relate to the Jewish tabernacle?

22. Every covenant involves the following actions: a call, a response, terms of the contract, sign of the agreement, and memorial established. Identify these elements in the Mosaic covenant; in a marriage contract.

Light from the New Testament

The New Covenant

God's desire to draw men into a LIFE-GIVING union with Himself depended on man's free response. The history of the covenant was one of man's repeated unfaithfulness. Since Christ Himself became the covenant, a mighty YES is continually being offered to the Father by all those who live in Him.

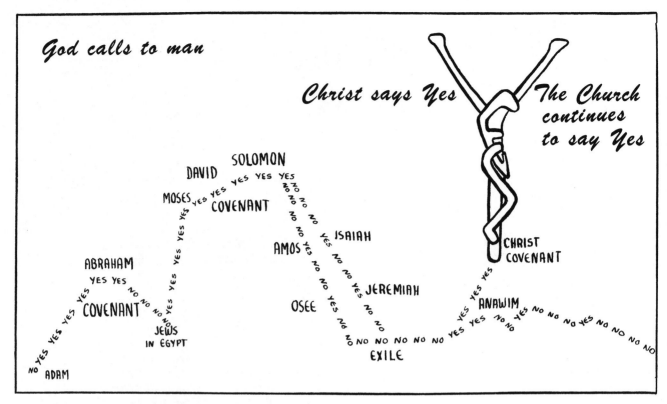

God calls to man

Christ says Yes

The Church continues to say Yes

SOLOMON
DAVID YES YES YES
MOSES YES YES YES
COVENANT

ISAIAH
AMOS

ABRAHAM
YES YES
COVENANT

CHRIST
COVENANT

JEREMIAH
OSEE

ANAWIM

JEWS
IN EGYPT

EXILE

NO ADAM

1. <u>Call</u> - <u>Matthew 3:13-17</u> - Jesus is anointed by the Holy Spirit for His saving mission.
2. <u>Response</u> - <u>2 Corinthians 1:19-22</u> - Jesus is the great "YES" to the Father for those who live in Him.
3. <u>Terms of Agreement</u> - <u>John 15:9-14</u> - LOVE--the Father, Christ, our brothers--as Jesus has loved us.
4. <u>Sign of Agreement</u> - <u>John 19:14-37</u> - The Blood of Christ

5. <u>Memorial</u> - <u>Matthew 26:26-28</u> - The Eucharistic Banquet

So You See...

Like the Israelites we have a covenant of friendship with God in Christ, so our standard of morality is concerned not so much with laws, as with the desire to please our Friend. The law helps us to know what pleases Him, but our love gives us the power to do it.

23. Sam has been chosen to go to West Point Academy. What difference will that make in the way he acts?

24. Donna is planning to get married soon. In order to prepare for her marriage, should she study books or her fiancé? Why?

25. If you had a friend who suddenly began to do things that were in complete opposition to standards basic to your friendship, would the friend eventually have to choose between you and these new practices?

To be holy, then, means to have come more and more to love the things that God loves--justice, honesty, kindness, reverence--and to hate the things that He hates. It does not consist in the fulfillment of many laws. Holiness is not DOING something--it is BEING something. It is living up to the greatest thing that could ever happen to you--God wanting to be your FRIEND.

The Terms of Your Covenant

By baptism you entered into a covenant with God. God called you into a living relationship with Him through Christ. Because your parents realized what a tremendous privilege it is to be associated with Christ, they wanted you to have it as soon as possible, and the Church accepted you at their request. But this relationship demands that you live in a manner befitting your high calling.

26. What obligations are imposed upon the family of the president of our country that could not have been demanded of them before the president took office?

27. Would you be fulfilling your obligations as a Christian if you lived by the standards of a good pagan? What more is required of you? Cf. First Epistle of St. John, Chapter 3

St. Paul (1 Corinthians 13:11) says, "When I was a child, I spoke as a child, I felt as a child, I thought as a child. Now that I have become a man I have put away the things of a child." Growing up in the Christian life demands that we "shift gears" in our moral life. Children need rules to guide them. Young people go behind the rules to see how they fit into the whole scheme of their "becoming." Mature adults go beyond the rules to find what love requires of them.

28. Discuss these two standards as guide lines for Christian decision. Apply them to various situations in your own life. The Sermon of the Mount (Matthew 5 and 6) may be helpful.

    a. What must I do to be saved?
    b. What can I do to please the Lord?

The Sign of Your Covenant

The Christian enters into this covenant by his baptism, where, like our Israelite ancestors, by the power of God's mighty intervention, he passes through water from slavery to freedom.

29. This is the story of the Exodus of the Israelites. Change the underlined words to make it the story of the Exodus of the Christians:

The Hebrews were led by Moses from the slavery of Egypt—saved by the blood of the Paschal Lamb and the passage through the waters of the Red Sea, led forward by a Luminous Cloud, nourished with Manna, and brought safely to the Promised Land.

St. Paul (Romans 6:3-4) says that the powerful act of God which makes our Passover possible is the Passover of His Son Jesus Christ (John 13:1). Every year when the Church commemorates the "blessed night" when God's saving power was exercised in our behalf, she invites her children to reaffirm their attachment to the Person of Christ by a renewal of their baptismal promises. This is an opportunity for you to do in your own name what was done for you by your godparents.

In the Easter Vigil she re-enacts the sacred drama of our initiation into Christ's life. The liturgical service revolves about the two signs, the Paschal candle and baptismal water—LIGHT and LIFE.

30. Read the "Exultet" of the Easter Vigil Service for a moving description of the Christian Exodus.

31. Explain what is symbolized by the light ceremony at the beginning of the service.

32. Using some of the symbols suggested by this service, design a card on which you copy a form for the renewal of your baptismal promises. Keep it in your prayerbook to use at appropriate times.

May a heavenly offspring, conceived in holiness, and born again a new creature, emerge from the stainless womb of the divine font

The Memorial of Your Covenant

Eating together has always been a sign of fellowship and a way of celebrating great events.

33. *Why does this experience of sharing food bring about a certain intimacy?*

34. *Show how a ceremonial meal was connected with:*
    a. the first Passover
    b. the signing of the Mosaic covenant
    c. Christ's Passover and the sealing of the New Covenant

The Mass, too, is a friendship meal in which all those who accept Christ join in celebrating their union with Him. Christ Himself becomes present at the Mass and His people unite with Him in sealing their covenant as God's faithful sons. At the close of the Canon, the people say AMEN (All that the Lord has said, we will do!) and then stand to say together, with the Beloved Son, "Our Father." The friendship bond with God is thus renewed and intensified.

The Eucharistic Banquet is God's pledge that all those who take part in it "shall eat and drink at My table in My kingdom." (Luke 22:30) With a blessing, the people are then sent out to <u>live</u> the promise they have pledged, to <u>give</u> the Christ they have received.

35. *What would you say of the disposition of the Christian, who, on Sunday, for no good reason, does not want to take part in this Meal that renews and celebrates our friendship with God? Cf. Matthew 22:1-14.*

It's Your Move!

1. *Describe the literary form of the Book of Exodus.*

2. *What is the significance of God revealing His name to Moses?*

3. *Discuss the relative merits of God's doing things in a spectacular way and working through very ordinary events.*

4. *Describe the Jewish Passover and give its significance.*

5. *What were the terms of the covenant God made with His people?*

6. *Explain the four qualities of the covenant.*

7. *Describe the ceremony by which the covenant was sealed and explain the symbolism.*

8. What was the Ark of the Covenant and what did it represent to the Jewish people?

9. What is the New Covenant? What are its terms, sign of agreement and memorial?

10. What is holiness?

11. What obligations came to you with your baptism?

12. Show how our moral life develops as we mature.

13. Show how the first Passover is a fitting symbol for Christ's passion and death and our baptism.

14. Describe the Easter Vigil Service.

15. What is the significance of the ceremonial meal in biblical history? Give some examples.

16. Show how the Mass is a renewal of our covenant and a ceremonial banquet.

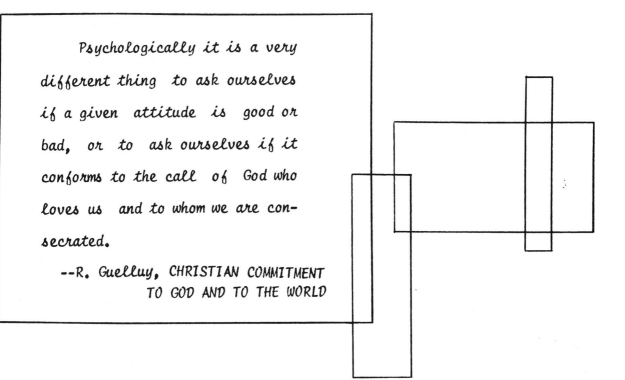

Psychologically it is a very different thing to ask ourselves if a given attitude is good or bad, or to ask ourselves if it conforms to the call of God who loves us and to whom we are consecrated.

--R. Guelluy, *CHRISTIAN COMMITMENT TO GOD AND TO THE WORLD*

Further Insights

Deuteronomy 4:32-40
5:22-7:25

The Book of Deuteronomy is something like an "inspired commentary" on the events of the Exodus. It has a strongly oratorical style as if it were a series of sermons of Moses. The purpose of the book seems to be to make the Israelites understand how much God loves them and how much He wants them to return that love. The writings of the New Testament have 112 allusions to Deuteronomy.

The Shema (Deut. 6:4-5) (Hebrew word for "hear") is a prayer which believing Jews still recite three times a day. The Hebrew profession of faith was a profound commitment to God, based on love of God for all that He had done for His people.

In the Catholic Biblical Encyclopedia (Old Testament), look up the words "mezuza" and "phylactery" (New Testament) for an explanation of how the Jews carried out the instruction in verse 8 and 9 of Chapter 4.

In the movie of that name, "Ben Hur," freed from galley chains, returns to find his home deserted. As he slowly opens the door of the empty house, he makes an odd gesture. Can you identify what it is? Do Catholics have a similar practice?

Comment on the passages in Matthew 23:5 and 22:36-39.

Reflection

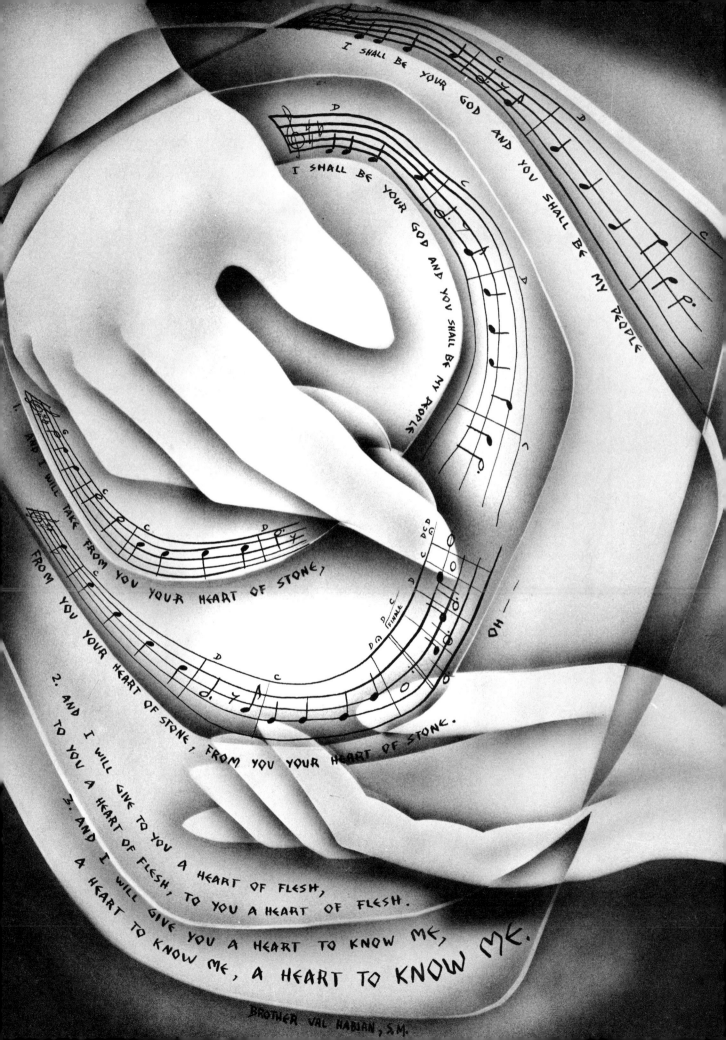

Chapter 6 -
God's Unshaken Fidelity

A Freshman Once Said
Is any friend true?

"Sure, I have friends--of a sort. But if I really got in a jam, I think they'd evaporate fast. You have to play it 'cool' and not expect too much of them. After all, let's face it, nobody's going to stick his neck out to stand by me. And I mean nobody!"

1. *What would you expect of a true friend?*

2. *What is involved in giving someone your word?*

3. *Are you ever justified in going back on your word?*

Light from the Old Testament

God had called His people from Egypt, broken the bonds that enslaved them and given His solemn word that He would never desert them. The people had given their word, too, but they found it very difficult to be faithful to it. Before they could take possession of the land that had been promised to them, they spent forty years in the desert learning what it means to be God's People. The Lord bore patiently with their bitter quarreling and their rebellious spirit and continued to "be their God."

God's Intimate Friend

When Moses went up into the mountain, the people persuaded Aaron, contrary to God's command, to let them make a golden bull to represent Yahweh's power and to be the center of their worship. (They had not yet been given the Ark of the Covenant.) They wanted a god like their neighbors had, one that they could see. Moses took advantage of God's love for him to obtain mercy for his people. For his sake, God relented and renewed the covenant.

4. What conditions are necessary in order to be a good mediator (go-between)? Apply these conditions to these situations:

Labor union	Arbitration board	Management
You	Mother	Father

5. Find some passages that show how close God's friendship with Moses was.

6. Find some passages that show how much Moses loved his people.

A Stiff-Necked...

Numbers 11 and 12

The Book of Numbers, as its name implies, tells about the organization of God's People during their 40 years in the desert. The theme that is repeated over and over is the failure of the people to obey and trust their leaders—God first and then Moses and the priests.

7. If you had been with the Israelites in the desert, would you have been one of those who sighed for "the good old days" in Egypt? Or would you have preferred to be free and not so safe and secure? Compare the situation in the desert to a life of faith.

...And Rebellious People

Numbers 13 and 14

When the spies came back from Chanaan and reported the prosperity and strong defenses they had seen there, the people refused to carry out the plan to invade it. Neither Joshua nor Caleb could persuade them that with God's help the invasion would be successful. They had much to learn before they would be fit instruments of God's power.

8. Why is it so important that we trust God?

"Joshua Fit...

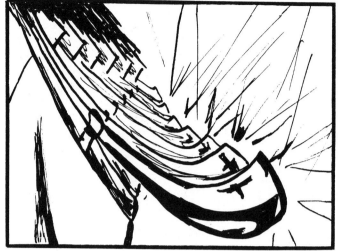

The Book of Joshua is the account of how God did, in fact, keep His word to Abraham and in a marvelous way bring His people into the Promised Land. It was a long and fierce campaign, for the Chanaanites saw the Israelites as a mob of barbarian nomads from the desert and they would not allow them to take over their land without a struggle, which continued off and on for 200 years.

9. Joshua had a motto which is repeated in Chapter 1 four times. It was one of President Kennedy's favorite quotations. Why was this an appropriate motto for both these men?

10. Joshua, or Jeshua, in English is "Jesus." St. Jerome said, "Joshua resembled Jesus in deeds as well as in name." Compare Joshua 1:6 with John 14:1-3 and Matthew 25:34 to find the similarity.

...De Battle of Jericho"

The whole description of the Battle of Jericho reminds one of a religious service with the priests and the Ark of the Covenant following the army. A providential earthquake has been suggested as the cause for the sudden collapse of Jericho's walls.

Among the ancients of the Near East, the institution of the "ban" was always linked with religious wars. According to this practice, the enemy, the city, its inhabitants, and their possessions were "dedicated" (that is, destroyed or slain) to the god who had given them victory. This was especially necessary for the Israelites to save them from religious and moral contamination with pagan religions. If it seems harsh, especially since it is attributed to God, it must be kept in mind that Joshua acted in accord with the custom of his day, and that his decisions would be regarded as coming from Yahweh through His chosen instrument.

11. Joshua is presented in the scriptural account as a "little Moses." Can you find some incidents that bring out the the similarity?

12. Learn the Negro spiritual "Joshua Fit de Battle of Jericho."

13. Is there anything in modern rules of warfare similar to the "ban"?

14. Some of the psalms (Ps. 136:7-9, for instance) also sound too blood-thirsty for our taste. We should think of the anger and strong feeling expressed in them as directed against the sin, although in the Semitic way of thinking and talking, the psalmist finds it difficult to distinguish between the sin and the sinner. Read Psalm 108, trying to share the writer's hatred of sin.

The Vicious Circle

Judges 2

The Book of Judges describes the same period of the Israelites history (1225 to 1025 B.C.) as does the Book of Joshua, but it emphasizes not so much the wonderful deeds of God as the frequent failures of the people to keep their covenanted pledge.

As the Israelites learned methods of agriculture from the native Chanaanites, they were often led to imitate their religious practices also. Chanaanite worship was a nature religion honoring the god and goddess of fertility by sexual practices that were forbidden to the Israelites. So, during this period, a certain pattern of action is repeated over and over again:
a. The Israelites adopted idolatrous practices
b. Yahweh allowed their enemies to press them hard
c. The people acknowledged their fault and pleaded for help
d. God inspired their leaders and their enemies were overcome.

These inspired leaders are called Judges, not because they were magistrates or rulers, but because they were signs of God's judgment on his people and of His call to repentance.

15. If your younger brother, in spite of everything you could do to talk him out of it, decides to go with a gang to break into a house, could it be a sign of love on your part to allow the gang to fall into the hands of the police? When God allows the Israelites' enemies to overcome them, is it an act of revenge or mercy? Give reason for your answer.

16. Does the pattern of action revealed in the lives of the Israelites exist in your life to some extent? Give an example.

Light from the New Testament

Our Middle Man

Just as Moses stood between God and the people as the link holding them together, so Christ is our bridge to the Heavenly Father. He is the perfect mediator because He is at the same time <u>one</u> with God and <u>one</u> with His people.

16. How does it feel to be a "go-between"? Is it easy? What can be achieved by someone who is willing to assume this role?

17. Discuss Our Lord's qualifications as mediator in the following passages:

    Matthew 17:1-8 - What expressions in the passage remind you of Moses (Exodus 34:30 and 33:17)?
    Hebrews 4:14-16 - What expression in the passage shows Christ's closeness to men?
    Luke 23:33-43 - Christ exercised His mediation in every act He performed as man, but His greatest act of mediation took place in the sacrifice of Himself on Calvary.
    Matthew 18:21-22 - Our Lord's answer to Peter tells us that there is no limit to the number of times we can call upon Christ's power of mediation.

So You See...

Even when you have reached the depths of misery, when you have been a total flop, when you're awkward and tongue-tied, and overweight and full of blotches, when you have struck out in the ninth inning with the winning run on third, when you have torn your sister's best blouse, when you are filled with remorse and disgust at having given in again, when, in a word, you are sure that you are utterly revolting--there is SOMEONE who loves you, just as you are, in all your misery and unhappiness. Christ loves you not because you deserve to be loved, but simply because you are YOU, and He reaches out to where you are to meet your need. And since His love does not depend upon your lovableness, there is nothing that can change it. He is utterly faithful.

66

Our Mountain of Mediation

Our altars are mountains of mediation. Every morning men go up these mountains and in their voices and in their gestures, Christ the Priest, offers Himself and us to the Father in a sacrifice of adoration, thanksgiving, reparation and petition. And then they come back to us bringing new life and strength, forgiveness and love from the Father. The priest is our external link with God as he exercises the internal mediation of Christ.

18. When we were baptized, we were given a share in Christ's priesthood. In what way can we be a link between our fellowmen and God? In what way can we be a link between God and our fellowmen?

19. Examine the Prayers of the Assembly at Mass. To whom are they addressed? How do they end? What conclusion would you draw from this?

TAKE

I have bread
    to break with you,
yet my hands are not oiled and bound

I have words
    to share with you,
yet my mouth opens not with sound.

I have Christ
    to give to you,
for Him in bread and word I found.

--Gretchen Meyer

It's Your Move!

1. Why did the Israelites remain in the desert for forty years?

2. Why did the people want a golden bull to worship?

3. What is necessary to be an effective mediator?

4. What is the theme of the Book of Numbers?

5. Explain the practice of the "ban" as used by the Israelites.

6. The Book of Joshua and the Book of Judges cover the same period of the Israelites history. Show how the two approaches differ.

7. To what great temptation were the Israelites exposed during this period?

8. What pattern of action developed as a result?

9. What is the role of the judges in salvation history?

10. Show how Christ is the perfect mediator with God.

11. What is the role of the priest in our relationship with God?

12. In what sense can all Christians be mediators?

Reflection

Prepare a Prayer of the Faithful for the class, using petitions made up from the thoughts considered in this chapter. For example:

That in all our difficulties and discouragement we may remember
    that God is faithful: we pray to the Lord.
        Response: Hear us, O Lord.

That we may all exercise the priesthood we received in baptism
    by bringing God to others: we pray to the Lord.
        Response: Hear us, O Lord.

Use this prayer from the Second Sunday in Lent, or any other that is appropriate, to close the service:

Let us pray. O Lord, you know that of ourselves we are powerless.
    Defend us inwardly and outwardly that our bodies may be guard-
    ed against all harm and our minds cleansed from evil thoughts:
    through our Lord Jesus Christ, Thy Son, who lives and reigns
    with You in the unity of the Holy Spirit, forever and ever.
Response: Amen.

Further Insights

Joshua 10:7-15

Stop the Sun!

Joshua's dramatic cry to the sun is a quotation from a book of patriotic songs, which celebrate the spectacular victories the Lord granted to Joshua. A too literal interpretation of this verse caused Galileo a great deal of trouble.

Mary Reed Newland in her book, THE FAMILY AND THE BIBLE (p. 69), describes a fascinating project that you might like to try, using your map on page 330 of your Bible as a pattern.

69

"Materials: a piece of scrap plywood from the lumber yard, wool and felt, straight pins and yarn. Covering the board with blue wool gave us background color for the water, and a surface on which to stick the individual pieces. Bright felt made each of the tribal portions, with an initial letter in contrasting color to identify each tribe. A piece of yarn made the Jordan. Straight pins helped to keep the pieces in place and made it possible to change the map to suit further history. As we worked, we reviewed what we had read so far, marked important places, named the patriarchs, their wives and children, and had an altogether satisfying review of the early history of God's people."

Agent 007

Joshua 2

Life in Jericho was exciting when rumors of the threatening invasion by the Israelites got around. The "shady lady" in the story turned out to be quite a person! You can find out more about her in these passages:

Hebrews 11:31   James 2:25   Matthew 1:5

God's Heroes

The Judges were men (and women) of their times. God used them to further His plan of salvation in spite of their defects. Cf. GOD'S WORD AND WORK (Sullivan) pages 51-74 for help in interpreting their lives.

Judges 3:12-30 - Aod, the left-handed one
Judges 4:1-24 - Debora, the prophetess
Judges 6:1-8:28 - Gedeon, the reluctant one
Judges 11:1-40 - Jephte, the juvenile delin-
                        quent
Judges 13:1 - 16:31 - Samson, the ladies' man

Chapter 7 - Salvation through God's People

A Freshman Once Said

Why do people need people?

"I can't think of anything worse than being 'out' of things. Have you ever walked up to a group and all of a sudden everybody 'clammed up' and changed the subject, or worse still, just melted away? It happened to me once, and I was never so miserable in all my life. I felt like an outcast, as if I had leprosy or something. And one week last summer everyone went on a vacation at the same time except me, and I was left to shift for myself. I had the tennis court, the pool, the records--but nothing was any fun. It seems as if we can't be happy without people."

1. *Show how much more men depend on others of their kind for physical survival than animals do. Is this dependence of men upon one another decreasing or increasing? Why is this so?*

2. *How do we depend on others intellectually?*

3. *Why is solitary confinement the worst of punishments?*

4. *Why is it so important to be accepted by people?*

Since our growth as a person is in direct proportion to our ability to believe, to trust, to love others, our personal development will depend to a great extent on our ability to "go out" to others to be transformed by these personal contacts. This is the role of the community.

The Bible calls David "a man after God's own heart" and gives an account of the transformation that was effected in him through his dealings with people, and of how God then used him to lay the foundation of a salvation community in the world.

Light from the Old Testament

Birth of the Kingdom

1 Kings 8-10

The first two Books of Kings (or the Books of Samuel) cover the century that is a turning point in the history of the people of God. Three men dominate the era: the saintly Samuel; Saul, "the man after the people's heart"; and David, "the man after God's heart." Cecil B. DeMille once said that he could make a movie out of every line in these books, which are a collection of popular narratives, eyewitness biographies, chronicles of the kings...and documents of the royal archives arranged in such a way as to give God's viewpoint on Israel's history.

Afraid of what might happen to them if they continued to lose to the Philistines, the people of Israel begged Samuel for a king to lead them against the enemy. At first, Samuel refused because it seemed to him that Israel was rejecting the Lord who had always been king of Israel. He warned them that kings would oppress them, but when they insisted, he anointed Saul of the tribe of Benjamin--a tall, handsome man and a courageous fighter.

> 5. *The Philistines were the natural enemies of the Israelites, different from them in every respect-- racial origins, language, religion, culture, and even physical stature. They were a formidable enemy who gave Palestine its name. They had discovered a secret which they guarded jealously (cf. 13:19-21.) and which gave them a great advantage over their more backward neighbors. Prepare a report for the class on these interesting people.*

To these ancient peoples the king was, in some way, a divine person. He was the sacred life-giving link between the people and their god. For the Hebrews, too, the king had a sacred character; he was the "Anointed of the Lord." But, unlike other kings of his time, he was not an absolute monarch, a law unto himself. He, too, was subject to the covenant and to the rebukes of the prophets.

> 6. *Read Deuteronomy 17:14-20 for a description of what was expected of the king.*

But Saul was self-willed. He disregarded Samuel's instructions and took things into his own hands. As a result, the kingship was taken away from Saul's family and given to another.

> 7. *In the light of what we know of God, would it be better to say that God rejected Saul or that Saul rejected God? Why?*

8. Tom saved his allowance for two weeks to buy his mother a birthday present but he consistently ignores her request to hang up his coat when he comes in. Quote some of Samuel's words to Saul that would be appropriate to his situation (cf. 1 Kings 15).

A Brave Leader

1 Kings 16 - The story of David's rise to fame begins in Bethlehem when Samuel, under the inspiration of the Lord, chooses from among Isai's (Jesse's) eight sturdy sons, the boy David to be the future king. Thus began a career in which two forces were constantly at work: recognition of the hidden will of God in the ordinary circumstances of life and the energetic use of every natural means to achieve that end. Until his last day David remained open to people and to God's action in his life and spontaneous in his response.

David became for future generations the ideal of what the king should be--strong and gentle, mighty and merciful, loving and faithful. He did much for his people; he won their loyalty and they always hoped that some day God would send them a ."Son of David" who would be like his father.

9. Which qualities of David made Saul love him and enabled him to relieve Saul's gloom and depression?

10. What does the Lord give as His reason for choosing David?

1 Kings 21:1 - 23:18-David's life as the fugitive leader of an outlaw band is full of human interest. Pretending to be on a royal errand, he secures food and a weapon from the high priest. He feigns madness to escape from the King of Geth. His nephews and the vagabonds of the area rally round him and they hire themselves out to the Philistines. Notice David's solicitude for his parents. (22:3)

11. Consult the Encyclopedic Dictionary of the Bible for more information about the ephod and the urim and thummin, their means of "consulting" the Lord.

2 Kings 3 - After Saul's death David was proclaimed King of Juda. Although the death of Abner removed an obstacle to his ascending the throne of Israel also, David grieved for Abner and publicly condemned the vengeance that had brought about his death.

12. Did David's refusal to take revenge detract from his reputation as a warrior? Contrast the impression of strength you received from the actions of Joab and those of David.

2 Kings 5 - David is anointed king of all Israel (about 998 B.C.).By a stroke of political genius he captured the Chanaanite city of Jerusalem and made it his capital. Strategically located on Mount Sion and made secure by its steep cliffs,the City of Peace was an ideal fortress for the King. David, familiar with the military tactics of the Philistines, was able to defeat them decisively,unify the country,and extend its boundaries.

13. *Read Psalm 86:1-7 and Luke 19:41-44 to discover how Jesus felt about the city of Jerusalem.*

14. *Why did the inhabitants of Jerusalem leave only the blind and the lame to guard the city?*

2 Kings 23:8-17 - David inspired intense devotion in his followers. The most famous warriors in his army, known simply as "The Three," risked their lives to get their leader a drink of water.

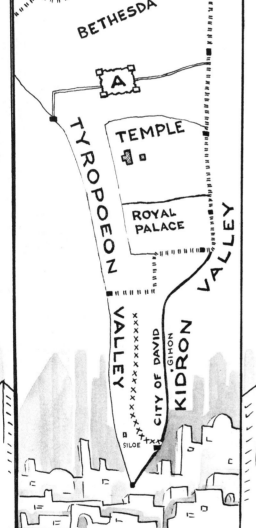

15. *What does David's refusal to drink the water the men brought to him at such a great cost reveal about his relationship to his men?*

A Devoted Follower

David was not a saint in the common understanding of the word,but he was deeply religious. He did not hesitate to satisfy his hunger w i t h the holy showbread when he was fleeing from Saul, because to him religion was not a set of rules of regulations but a personal attachment to God to whom he bound himself in a living commitment.

16. *Read Psalm 50: 18-19 and 1 Kings 16:7 and compare David's idea of religion with God's idea of David.*

1 Kings 17 - The story of David and Goliath is a colorful illustration of how David relied on God, and of how God was with David in all that he did. The Chosen People often in their later history needed this example of reliance on God; they were more inclined to depend on the force of arms and on alliances with powerful nations.

17. David's philosophy of life is expressed very concisely in these words to Goliath: "The Lord will deliver thee into my hand, and I will slay thee." What do they mean? Make a slogan for David that will express the same idea.

1 Kings 26 - Although Saul pursued David relentlessly for several years in an effort to kill him, David refused to take advantage of the opportunity he had to kill Saul. Note how the occasion brings out the calm self-possession of David and his profound respect for the king as the "Lord's Anointed."

18. Many people would say David was a fool for not "taking care" of Saul when he had the chance; others say it was a sign of true greatness. What do you say?

19. Sometimes we, like David, are required to show respect for the office a person holds, even though we cannot honestly respect the person who holds the office. Give some examples of this.

20. What does verse 20 tell you about David? Do you like him more for this quality?

21. Of which phrase of the Our Father does verse 24 remind you?

DAVID

Against Goliath of Geth
    from the stream of eternity,

I have five smooth stones
    to throw

Which will be the death
    of me.
            --Gretchen Meyer

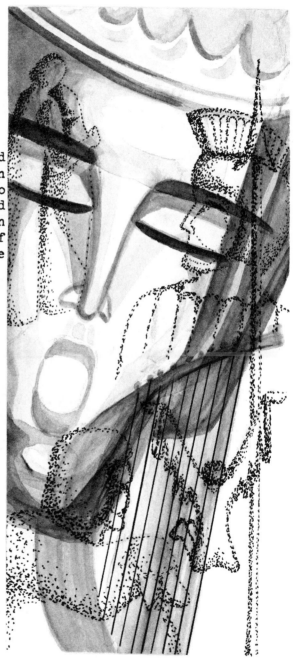

2 Kings 6 - By bringing the Ark into Jerusalem, the capital, David acknowledged that the Covenant was the foundation of their existence as a people, that the Lord was now a king enthroned on Mount Sion, and that the king of Israel was the representative. The whole chapter highlights the reverence due to the Ark, which was the sign of God's presence among His people.

22. Why has Jerusalem become the symbol both of the Church and of the heavenly kingdom?

23. Psalm 23 was probably composed for this occasion. Recite the psalm in class with a selected group asking the questions in verses 3, 8, and 10. As you read the psalm, try to share David's sentiments as he danced before the Ark. Would this be an appropriate psalm to sing at Sunday Mass?

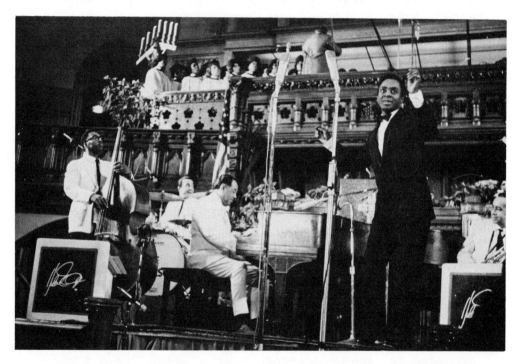

Tapping out "David Danced Before the Lord With All His Might," Bunny Briggs "talks" to the Lord during Duke Ellington's Concert of Sacred Music at the Fifth Avenue Presbyterian Church in New York City. Citing Psalm 150, the Pastor said:
Praise God in his sanctuary....
Praise him with the sound of the trumpet....
Praise him with the timbrel and dance.

24. Michol, David's wife, ridiculed his religious practices. Their differences became an insurmountable barrier in their relationship. Discuss this problem in terms of people today.

A Loyal Friend

1 Kings 18: 1 - 9
19: 1 - 17
20: 1 - 43
23:15 - 18

The friendship between David and Jonathan is one of the most beautiful relationships in literature. Jonathan was even willing to renounce his claim to the throne in favor of his friend. Each new persecution of David by Jonathan's father merely served as an occasion for them to renew their covenant with each other.

25. The capacity for true friendship makes one more warmly human. Show how the love between David and Jonathan had the qualities of true friendship by quoting the verses that illustrate these characteristics:

    a. A friend thinks more of his friend's good than of his own.

    b. A friend loves his friend as himself.

    c. A friend helps another to grow.

    d. A friend is a support in bearing the difficulties of life.

    e. Friends owe loyalty to each other.

2 Kings 1 - David's famous lament over the slain Saul and Jonathan portray both his gift of poetry and his generous love. The harsh treatment he had endured at the hands of Saul served but to refine and mature his character and never succeeded in making him bitter.

26. What connection, if any, is there between David's ability to love Jonathan and his ability to love God?

27. Read 2 Kings 9 to see how David kept his word to Jonathan.

A Royal Sinner

2 Kings 11:1 - 12:25

But in the stress of temptation the great king was as weak as his least subject. He committed adultery and,in order to avoid discovery,cunningly arranged to have Urias murdered. It is a shattering moment when a good man is brought face to face with his crime, but David was humble enough to admit his guilt and to seek God's healing mercy for his wound.

28. The sincerity of David's repentance is evident in the patience with which he bore the tragedy that marked his family life from that day. Read 2 Kings 16:5-14 for an example of this.

29. When Nathan said, "Thou art THE MAN!", David had a moment of REALIZATION. Try to imagine the **conflicting** thoughts that struggled for the possession of David's mind at that moment. Write the conversation in which David tries to share this moment with Bathsheba.

30. What is the only thing that is worse than sin?

Forgiving, he forgave almost foolishly; sorrowing, he was inconsolable; loving, he was heartbreakingly tender; and angry, he was vicious.

--Mary Reed Newland, THE FAMILY AND THE BIBLE

A Forgiving Father   2 Kings 15 and 18:1 - 19:8

David's favorite son, Absalom, handsome and impulsive like his father, organized a revolt by which he hoped to seize control of the kingdom. David, on foot and in tears, leaving even the Ark behind, fled from Jerusalem. In this unhappy situation we see David at his best, abandoned by his people, but enriched by all his contacts with them and with God, accepting the sorrow but continuing to use all the resources at hand to end the rebellion. When Absalom was killed contrary to his orders, David was inconsolable.

31. Compare John 18:1-9 and 2 Kings 15:23 and 30-34.

32. These are tributes paid to President Kennedy. Describe incidents in which David displayed these same qualities.

He had that special grace--in so many ways.

He was a <u>graceful</u> man, physically graceful in his movements and had that special grace of the intellect that is taste.

He was a <u>restless, exuberant</u> man, always looking forward to the next <u>challenge</u>.

He was a <u>leader</u> who gained the admiration, trust, and affection of <u>those</u> whom he led--resolute without being arrogant, patient without being timid, and compassionate without being maudlin.

He was a <u>loving</u> man--loving his country and his people with a <u>tribal love</u>. His heart leapt up when he saw his son.

He was a <u>forgiving</u> man, far more forgiving than his friends. He <u>forgave quickly</u> and for good, and soon found new quality in the one <u>forgiven</u>.

He was a <u>wonderfully funny</u> man, always gay and cheerful, never mean. He never seemed dismayed for long by misfortune. He bore his burdens with courage and vitality and met his challenges with hope.

The House that God Built

2 Kings 7

Everything that was written about David was written for the sake of the message God gave him through the prophet N a t h a n. Having compared his palace with the crude tent that housed the Ark, David wished to build the Lord a house (that is, a temple). But the Lord proposed instead that He build David a house (that is, a dynasty) that would last forever.

In other words, God revealed that He would be present to men not so much in a material building as in a community of people to whom He would give H i s word and His presence. The community would be formed around David's descendants; they would preserve and communicate what they had received without fail for endless ages. David recognized that by this promise God had renewed the Covenant in a special way with his family so that His saving action would be exercised under their leadership.

33. *Show how the promise to David was merely a new development of the promise made to Abraham.*

34. *What does this promise have to do with you today?*

35. *C h o o s e appropriate verses from Psalm 17, David's prayer of thanksgiving, to be used as the prayer before or after class.*

Life is fellowship. Lack of fellowship is equivalent to death. Heaven, too, is fellowship, and lack of it is hell. (McGarrigle, TWO COMMANDMENTS OF CHRIST)

Son of David

The glorious kingdom of David soon crumbled as one faithless king after another occupied the throne. But the prophets reaffirmed t h e promise of Nathan that there would come a son of David who would, like David, be God's own son and through his fidelity the blessings of the Covenant would come to all his people.

John 7:40-42 - Even when they were under the power of Rome, the people continued to hope for the great king of David's line.

Matthew 1:1, Mark 10:47-48, **Luke 1: 32-33** - The **evangelists** proclaim Jesus as the long-awaited son of David.

John 18:33-37 and 19:19-22 - Jesus claims kingship but establishes the spiritual nature of His kingdom. He dies in defense of His claim.

Acts 13:16-34 - Paul relates the giving of the promise and its fulfillment in Christ.

36. Can you answer the Pharisees' question (Matthew 22:41-46) as to how Christ could be both "the Son of David" and the "Lord of David"?

Matthew 13:24-30 - By means of a parable Our Lord tells us that until He comes again, His kingdom, in which we find salvation, will be composed of people good and not so good, and that in them we will find both His Word and His Presence.

37. Why does God choose to come to us through other people rather than through a more direct means? Does this mean that we must go to God the same way?

So You See...   We Need Each Other

Just as we are materially, intellectually, and socially dependent upon others for our full human development, so we are spiritually dependent upon them also. We are saved not as individuals, but because we are joined to the community of believers in whom Christ is present. The bond of faith will not unite us to Christ unless we are united by the bond of charity to our brothers. WE NEED EACH OTHER.

38. LISA AND DAVID (Theodore Isaac Rubin, Ballantine Books, New York, 1963) is the true story of two mentally ill adolescents who have built walls around themselves and who desperately need to escape from them into the real world of human relations. Discuss why people withdraw from others and what happens if no one can reach them. If you limit your association to a few people, do you thereby limit your development as a person?

Anointed for Worship

Olive oil was produced in great quantities in Palestine and had many uses both sacred and profane:

<u>Cosmetic</u>--to protect against the sun, to soothe and refresh.
<u>Medicinal</u>--to heal sores and wounds.
<u>Religious</u>--to show consecration to God and the bestowal of a certain office, especially that of kingship and priesthood. It was a sign of the gift of Yahweh's spirit and the king was referred to as "the Messiah," the "Anointed of the Lord."

39. Show which of these traditional uses of oil are symbolized in the anointings which take place in the sacraments of baptism, confirmation, holy orders and the anointing of the sick.

When the "anointed of the Lord" offer their worship today, they do so, not as individuals, but as the community of God's People united in Christ.

40. Examine the prayers of the Mass for the use of "I" and "we," "me" and "us." What do you conclude from this?

> Because heaven will be the revelation of love, love that really deserves the name, it will bring about at the same time the fullest development both of personality and of community. There my happiness will be more than ever mine, God will be more than ever my God; yet no one will say "my God," "my happiness"; it will be "our God," "our happiness."
>
> --Yves Congar, THE WIDE WORLD MY PARISH

It's Your Move!

1. Show how we depend on others physically, intellectually and socially.

2. What is the content and the literary form of the Books of Samuel?

3. Give the pro and con of Israel's having a king.

4. Compare the concept of kingship in Israel with that of other nations of the same era.

5. What characterized David's approach to life?

6. Why was David able to inspire such loyalty in his followers?

7. Cite instances from David's life to illustrate his genuine commitment to God.

8. Give the characteristics of true friendship and show how the possession of these enables a person to love God.

9. Show how the realization of his weakness made David a better person.

10. What is the best proof of the sincerity of David's repentance?

11. What new element of God's promise to Abraham is revealed in His promise of an everlasting dynasty to David?

12. How was the promise to David fulfilled?

13. Explain the role of the community in the saving work of God.

Reflection   Who Is the Other?

"The other--whomever you meet on the road of life...the one to whom you must unite yourself in love to become fully a man by being a brother to all--the one to whom you must unite yourself in love if you would make a success of your life and join in the movement of universal salvation won in Jesus Christ."

--Michel Quoist, THE MEANING OF SUCCESS

Further Insights

Speak, Lord...

1 Kings 1-3--Marvelous stories surround Samuel's birth from Anna (once thought sterile), his fidelity, and his fame that grew from day to day until he became a spiritual giant among the Israelites. He was not merely the high priest but a prophet and the last of the Judges.

The First Robin Hood

1 Kings 25 - An intriguing "tale of an outlaw chieftain who woos and wins a beautiful lady on the death of her ugly husband," as Mary Reed Newland so deftly says in THE FAMILY AND THE BIBLE. Abigail testifies to David's reputation for justice and forebearance.

Macbeth in the Old Testament

1 Kings 28 - Saul give a frightening picture of the man who, though called by God to a high mission, chooses to "do it his way." He tries to make contact with God through a witch but succeeds only in hearing his doom pronounced.

Chapter 8 - The Worship of God's People

A Freshman Once Said
Where are you, God?

"I've heard so much about you and I'd really like to meet you. But how does one meet a spirit? Sometimes I pray and I think you listen to me way up there. But heaven is so far away. They say you're everywhere, but practically speaking, someone who is everywhere seems to be nowhere. And then I go to Mass and I should find you there, but the people get in my way and somehow we never quite make connections. I'm sure if I could just meet you sometime it would be easy to love you."

Perhaps you have never thought about it, but there is a difference between being located in a certain place and being "present" there.

1. Explain how you can be "located" at your desk in school but not "present" there.

Only a spirit can be present, material things have location. Men have location insofar as they have bodies, and presence insofar as they have spiritual powers. Persons are present to each other when they are deliberately aware of each other and able and willing to communicate.

2. Can anyone force you to be in a certain location? Can you be forced to be "present" to anyone? What does that tell you about presence?

3. Can you be present to someone who is not present to you? What does that tell you about presence?

4. Are we concerned about where God is "located" or where He is "present"?

Light from the Old Testament
God Comes to the Patriarchs

When God first became present to men by their response of faith, they tended to connect His presence with the place where they were at the time. They set up markers at the places sanctified by this meeting with God and went back there to renew their contact with Him.

Genesis 12:7-8; 13:3-4 and 18 - Abraham seems to have thought of God as located in these places and the altar is the means of communicating with Him.

Genesis 28:10-22 - Here God renewed the covenant with Jacob, who then marked the place where He and God had been present to each other.

5. Consult the Encyclopedic Dictionary of the Bible for a more detailed explanation of the symbolism of the altar.

God Dwells Among His People

For the **patriarchs** their meeting with God was a memory often renewed, but God wanted it to be a way of life. He set about trying to teach man that he is not alone in the world, that God is at work in everything that happens to him, that He wants to live in their hearts and to speak to them.

Exodus 25:21-22 - By means of the Covenant God and His people pledge their mutual fidelity and the sign of the Covenant becomes the sign of God's presence with His people.

Exodus 29:42-46 and 33:7-17 - Unlike the Patriarchs who had to go to the holy places to find God, the Israelites had God dwelling with them. The Tent was the meeting place of God and man.

Deuteronomy 4:29-31 - But God is not interested primarily in places; He is interested in fidelity and love. He draws near to Israel, always ready to communicate with her, but His presence depends on Israel's fidelity and readiness to respond in faith and trust.

6. Discuss the words: "You shall indeed find Him when you search after Him with your whole heart and your whole soul" (Deut. 4:29). How can you "search after" God?

The Sign of God's Presence

3 Kings 8: 1 - 30
8:54 - 9:9

When David asked to build God a temple, God made it clear that what counts is not so much the existence of an official dwelling-place, as the fact of His presence in the hearts of His people. But the people in whom God was present wanted a special place in which His presence would be visibly manifested by the magnificence of its furnishings and the splendor of its ceremonies. They would learn to their sorrow that it was not the Temple building but the inner dispositions of their hearts that guaranteed God's presence among them.

7. From the biblical description (2 Paralipomenon 3 and 4), draw a floor-plan of Solomon's temple. Mark the dimensions (a cubit is equal to the distances from the elbow to the tip of the middle finger--about 18 inches). Locate and identify the main furnishings.

8. Consult the Encyclopedic Dictionary of the Bible for information about the three **temples** that succeeded each other in Jerusalem.

Man in God's Presence

When man meets God, he instinctively falls "prostrate with his face to the ground in worship." Worship is MAN'S RESPONSE TO GOD'S REVELATION OF HIMSELF. It is rooted in the realization that he depends on God for all that he is and has and in the inner acceptance of that dependence. A man who does not willingly subject his mind and heart to God is building his life on a very uncertain foundation.

9. Of all God's creatures only man is capable of worshipping his Maker. Why?

10. Dave claims that he taught his parrot to pray the "Our Father." His friend Jack says that such a thing is impossible. With whom do you agree? Would God be honored by the parrot's "prayer"? How many of your prayers are "parrot" prayers?

Signs of Worship

Although worship begins in the heart, if it stays there, it is not completely human. It is natural for human beings to express their thoughts and feeling, especially their feelings about God. In order to make our encounter with God more impressive and more effective, we make use of words and gestures, persons and things, poetry and music. The use of external signs serves a two-fold purpose: 1. To express what is in the soul, and 2. To evoke and strengthen those sentiments.

11. What devices are used to express and foster the "will to win" at a football game? Are they effective in arousing enthusiasm? Does this apply also to the expression of religious feeling?

12. Consult Romano Guardini's Sacred Signs for material on the various common gestures used in worship: folding hands, kneeling, standing, walking, striking the breast.

Religious gestures make the worship of God beautiful, orderly, and impressive, but they are empty signs unless they are the external expression of interior devotion. Resolve to make all the sacred signs you use really stand for something within you.

14. Give some examples of how people are content to let their religion consist in the exact use of exterior signs without any concern for the reality for which they are supposed to stand.

All You Works of the Lord...

Although inanimate creatures of themselves cannot praise God, they can participate in man's worship and in this way attain their highest fulfillment.

15. Consult Exodus 25:1-8 for a list of material things used in Temple worship. Show how most of them are still used in worship today.

16. In what sense can man be called the "priest of the universe"?

17. In the Book of Daniel (3:57-90) the three young men in the fiery furnace call upon all the wonders of nature to "bless the Lord." Write a similar prayer in which you call upon all the wonders of our technological and scientific age to "bless the Lord."

With One Voice

Sirach 50:5 - 21

God had made the Israelites into a people--His People--and revealed Himself to them as their God. The saving events of their history had not been for any individual, but for the people. It was fitting, therefore, that the people should respond to Him not merely as individuals but as the community to which God had revealed Himself.

When people express themselves publicly as a group, it is necessary to set up a definite pattern of word and action. This public and official expression of the worship of God's People is called the LITURGY. It is the two-way communication by which God makes Himself present to His people, offering them salvation, and they respond with love and devotion.

18. Discuss: "God calls a people to remake shattered mankind into a single family centered about its Father."

19. Individuals are formed into a community through sharing common experiences, similar ideals, and the same destiny. Show how this is true in the case of a family, of America, of the Red Cross Organization, and of the Democratic Party. What were the unifying forces that made Israel a people? What are the benefits of the community worshipping together?

20. In the following assemblies some are simply groups of people, while others form true communities. Discuss the factors that contribute to ONENESS and name the groups which seem to have unity:

   a. Passengers in a train

   b. Musicians in an orchestra

   c. Students' assembly on Awards Day

   d. Crowd at the rush hour

   e. Actors in a play

   f. Family at mealtime

   g. Congregation at Holy Mass

21. Do you think that the American way of life gives moral encouragement to a spirit of individualism or to a community spirit? Why?

Worship through Feasts

The observance of feasts became for the People of God occasions for recalling the great acts of God in their behalf--creation, the deliverance from Egypt, the giving of the Law, and His care for them in the desert. And because he was one with his people, each individual felt that he not only celebrated the historic event, but that he actually took part in it. He could relive what his ancestors had experienced because the mighty deeds of God continued to be exercised in behalf of him and of his people. As he relived the past and rejoiced in the present, he hoped with great confidence for God's mercy and protection in all the events of the future.

22. Show how the celebration of your birthday involves the past, the present, and the future.

The main feasts of Israel have with some changes passed over into the Christian calendar also. Our feasts, like theirs, revolve around the great saving acts of God for His people.

Feasts of
The Old Israel   The New Israel

The Sabbath

Celebrated on the last day of the week. Commemorated creation of the world.

Sunday

Celebrated on the first day of the week. Commemorates the New Creation that took place in the Resurrection and the Descent of the Holy Spirit.

The Passover

Celebrated in April (first full moon after the spring equinox). Commemorated the Exodus, the passing from slavery to freedom.

Easter

Celebrated the Sunday following the first full moon after the spring equinox. Commemorates the Exodus of Christ, by which we pass from the slavery of sin to newness of life in Christ.

Pentecost

Celebrated 50 days after the Passover. Commemorated the giving of the Law on Mount Sinai -- the Covenant, which brought forth the People of God.

Pentecost

Celebrated 50 days after Easter. Commemorates the establishment of the New People of God by the giving of the Holy Spirit.

Feast of Tents

Celebrated for 7 days in the seventh month. Commemorated the sojourn in the desert and God's care of His People; gratitude for the grape and olive harvest.

The Eucharist

Celebrated daily. Official giving of thanks for God's provident care in our journey to the Promised Land.

Feast of Atonement
(Yom Kippur)

Celebrated t h e tenth day of seventh month. Day of penance and confession of sins. Scapegoat ceremony.

Good Friday

Celebrated Friday before Easter. Commemorates the death of Our Savior "who takes away the sins of the world."

Feast of Lights
(Hanukkah)

Celebrated 25th day of ninth month. Commemorated rededication o f the Temple.

Christmas

Celebrated on December 25. Commemorates t h e birth of the Light of the World, the N e w Meeting Place of God and Man.

23. *The Book of Leviticus, chapters 16 and 23, and Exodus, chapter 12, contain the regulations for observing these feasts. Prepare a report for the class on them. Ask a Jewish friend to tell you how these feasts are observed today.*

24. *Jesus observed these feasts with His people. Look up these references in the Gospel: John 10:22, John 7:1-15, Luke 22: 1-20.*

Worship through Sacrifice
Leviticus 6:1 - 7:22

Sacrifices were gifts acknowledging the lordship of God and putting the sacrificer entirely at His service. By his gift the worshipper manifested his desire to enter the presence of Yahweh to be united with Him. When part of the offering was returned to the offerer, he held a "love-feast" with his friends, at which God was considered to be a guest. This sacred meal renewed the bonds of the Covenant between the Lord and the other guests.

The law of the Old Testament laid down detailed regulations for the sacrificial procedure. There were four main kinds of sacrifices offered in the Temple.

a. Holocaust - t h e victim was entirely burned to show m a n's complete submission. (Adoration)

b. Cereal oblation - "first fruits" of the harvest; no laymen ever allowed to share in it. (Thanksgiving)

c. Peace offering - always an animal; part burned and part served at banquet. (Thanksgiving)

d. Sin offering - an animal; offered to atone for sins of weakness and to effect "at-one-ment." (Reparation)

25. *We sometimes use the word "sacrifice" to refer to acts of mortification. How is this use of the word different from, and similar to, the more general meaning?*

Worship through Prayer

The form of worship that is available to us everywhere and always is prayer. We are always welcome in God's presence. Whether our prayer is public or private, formal or informal, the first great requirement is sincerity. Each of us must come to God as he is. Nothing is so out of place as "playing the role" with God.

26. Sometimes the outdated English used in prayer formulas gets in the way of our really praying. Study this version of the Our Father. Does it make the Lord's Prayer more meaningful for you?

"Our Father living in heaven
How wonderful you are!
May your plans for this world really come true!
May things happen here on earth the way You want them to,
    just as they do in heaven.
Please give us all that we need to live a full life.
And don't hold our mistakes against us,
Just as we promise not to hold other people's mistakes
    against them.
Don't let our weaknesses get the better of us,
But give us your strength."

--Brother J. Frederick and Brother H. Albert, TO LIVE IS CHRIST

Translate the Hail Mary into your own language.

The Psalms

The psalms beautifully capture the deep personal faith of the Old Testament man. They spring from the profound realization of the greatness of God and of His goodness. In language that is always noble and inspired, they sing the praise of God, thank Him for His great mercy and beg with confidence for His continued care. Because they spring from the human situations of God's People, they fit all our prayer needs. But while they express a wide range of intensely personal feeling toward God, there is no "gushy" emotionalism nor "sugary" piety in them.

From the time of David (who organized the Temple worship and wrote some of the psalms) the Psalter has served as the prayer book of the People of God in both the Old and the New Testament.

27. There are several hundred references to the psalms in the Gospels alone. Check the seven last words of Our Lord on the cross to find how many of them are quotations from the psalms.

28. Which psalms are used in the Ordinary of the Mass? Which parts of the propers of the Mass are composed of psalms?

92

29. Learn some of the musical settings of the psalms by Father Joseph Gelineau, S.J.

The Rhythm of Thought

The psalms are Hebrew poetry, originally sung to the accompaniment of a stringed instrument. But they are not the rhyming, metered poetry that we are used to. In Hebrew poetry, meaning plays a far greater role than sound, so instead of sound patterns, there are thought patterns in which two successive lines, or parts of a line, repeat or re-enforce the first idea. This is called parallelism. For example:

"My steps have been steadfast in your paths, my feet have not faltered." (Psalm 16:5)

"Turn away your face from my sins, and blot out all my guilt." (Psalm 50:11)

You will like the magnificent word-pictures of the psalms, which en-kindle the imagination and stir the emotions and make you want to think about them. This is called concreteness. For example:

"In the shadow of your wings I take refuge, till harm pass by." (Psalm 56:2)

"As the hind longs for the running waters, so my soul longs for you, O God." (Psalm 41:2)

30. Read Psalms 17 and 103 for examples of concreteness. Choose some very vivid passages and tell in your own words the thought or emotion that they evoke.

31. Read Psalms 58 and 37 for examples of parallelism.

Odes to the King

The Psalter contains a number of "royal" hymns written to, or about, the king. But the reigning king was only a shadow of the great King-to-come, the promised Son of David, and the poems composed for his enthrone-ment came to have a meaning far beyond the original reference. They are called Messianic psalms.

32. Read Psalms 2, 44, 71, 109. What references in them could be applied to Christ?

Praying the Psalms

The faithful of the Old Testament knew and loved the psalms. The gospels give evidence that Jesus and Mary and the Apostles had absorbed both their spirit and their style of expression. The psalms reflect our hopes and aspirations, too, and can become for us a very meaningful form of prayer, if we:

a. Read the psalm slowly and carefully to provide the necessary transition from the world of pressure and activity to the calm world of the spirit and of God. Say it aloud if possible. Dwell on the words.

b. Identify its spirit--praise, lament, thanksgiving, petition. Think of its meaning: when it was written; in terms of Christ; in terms of myself as a living member of Christ's Body.

c. Talk to God about it.

33. One way of making the psalms our own is to use them frequently as our personal prayers. Make a booklet of the verses that appeal to you most and give them a title, such as, "Prayer before Confession," "Morning Prayer," "Prayer after a Failure," "Prayer in Temptation," etc.

Even as merely human documents, the psalms deserve attention as classic compositions of the human spirit as it turns to God. Within the pages of the Psalter, mankind lays bare its soul.... But much more than that, the psalms breathe with the very life of God's People.
-Vincent M. Novak, S.J., from JESUS CHRIST, OUR LIFE AND WORSHIP

Light from the New Testament

...In Spirit and in Truth

God's drawing near to His People in the Old Testament reaches its climax when He comes to dwell among us in the person of His Son Jesus Christ. In Him God has both "location" and "presence." Jeremias (7:1-15) had warned the people that because of their unfaithfulness, God would withdraw His presence from the Temple; nevertheless, Ezechiel reaffirms His promise to "set up His sanctuary among them FOREVER." Both these prophecies came true in a very wonderful way.

John 4:21-24 - Jesus raises the question of the Temple and true worship and says that God's inner presence would be manifested in a material way.

Matthew 12:6 - Christ told the Pharisees that although the Lord was present in their magnificent Temple, He was present in a more perfect manner in Himself.

Matthew 24:2 - He does not hesitate to say that the beautiful Temple, the meeting place with God, would be utterly destroyed.

John 2:13-22 - John explains the mysterious words of the Lord and helps us to realize that although both Temples would be destroyed, only one, the Body-Temple of Jesus, would be "rebuilt" at the Resurrection.

Matthew 27:51 - With the completion of Christ's sacrifice, the Hebrew liturgy was replaced by the new liturgy in the New Temple.

> 34. *Martha's husband died several months ago and she misses him very much. Sometimes to ease the loneliness she goes to Church and kneels in the place he used to occupy, and sometimes she sits at home with her five-year old son on her lap. Which better conveys a sense of presence, a place or a person? Why? With regard to God's presence among us why are we more fortunate than the Jews of the Old Testament?*

Christ Present in Our Flesh

When David wanted to build a temple, God said, "No! let Me build you a family instead." And when the Risen Christ took His place at the right Hand of the Father, He sent His Spirit into the People of God so that until the end of time the "Word was made flesh" in us. Today Christ is present to us through the Body, which is the Church. Thus, the Church is the saving Presence of Jesus Christ in the world, but WE ARE THE CHURCH.

> 35. *If it is through men that God chooses to communicate His salvation to other men, what does this mean for us?*

"Abide in me, and I in you. As the branch cannot bear fruit of itself unless it remain on the vine, so neither can you unless you abide in me. I am the vine, you are the branches. He who abides in me, and I in him, he bears much fruit; for without me you can do nothing."

John 15:4-5

So You See...

God is not far away; He is in your heart and to meet Him you have only to make yourself present to Him there. And more than this, Christ has become incarnate in the Church, the People of God, and we can meet Him in the official acts of the liturgy and in the personal contacts we have with one another. We bring Christ to others and they bring Him to us.

"It belongs to the Church to be at the same time human and divine, visible and rich in invisible realities, fervent in action and occupied with contemplation, present in the world and yet alien to it. In such a way what is human in her is directed toward what is divine, the visible toward the invisible, action toward contemplation, the present toward the future city which we seek. Thus, since every day the liturgy builds up those who are in the Church in order to make them a holy Temple in the Lord, a dwelling of God in the Spirit, until the size corresponding to the fullness of Christ is reached, it also in an amazing way, strengthens their energies to make them proclaim Christ."

--G. Tavard, THE PRESENCE OF GOD

The Most Perfect Encounter

- Hebrews 9:11 - 28

Sacrifice is the highest act of worship, and the sacrifice of Christ is the supreme act of sacrifice. Christ expressed the most perfect sentiments of love and submission to His Father by His painful and bloody death on Calvary. But His love for the Father is an eternal act of intense devotion. In every Mass He uses not His bloody death, but bread and wine to express that love. This is the same bread and wine that is also the sign of our love and submission. So in the Mass, Christ offers Himself and us, and we offer ourselves and Christ in one act of love and dedication to the Heavenly Father. The Mass, therefore, is the sacrificial gift by which we renew our covenant with the Lord.

36. Examine the prayers of the Canon of the Mass that are said after the Consecration and pick out the phrases by which the priest makes this offering.

37. The Canon ends with the "Great Amen," by which the people signify their desire to ratify the offering personally. What change was made in the new liturgy to make this moment of the Mass more impressive?

When we have committed ourselves to God and His cause, Jesus comes to us personally in the closest union we can imagine. The sign of this union is the act of eating and its effect is to draw us ever more deeply into the redemptive power of Christ and to bring about our gradual transforma-tion.

38. Why is the act of eating an apt sign for the close union it represents?

39. The liturgical sign has three dimensions: past, present and future. Show how the banquet sign of the Eucharist was fore-shadowed in the Old Testament and will be fulfilled in the future. Cf. Exodus 12:21-28 and Apocalypse 19:7,9.

40. When we receive Christ's body in Holy Communion, we receive it in the state in which it is NOW. In which state is that?

41. Discuss: The union we share in the Mass must be both vertical and horizontal.

It's Your Move!

1. What does it mean to be present to someone?

2. What did the patriarchs do to renew God's presence among them?

3. After the Exodus what new development took place with regard to God's presence?

4. Why did the people want a sign of God's presence among them?

5. What is worship?

6. Why do we use signs to express our worship? What danger is involved in this?

7. What is the liturgy?

8. What principles are involved in forming a community of people?

9. What is the purpose of observing feasts? What should be the disposition of those observing them?

10. Compare the feasts celebrated by the Old and the New Israel.

11. What dispositions on the part of the offerer did the sacrificial gift represent?

12. What is the most important quality of prayer?

13. Describe the spirit of the psalms.

14. Explain the characteristics of Hebrew poetry.

15. Why is Jesus called the "New Temple"?

16. How is Christ present to us today?

17. Describe the sacrificial action of the Mass.

18. Show how the liturgical sign of the Eucharist has three dimensions

Reflection

REFLECTION: If here at the Christian altar one lifts up to God his small piece of world together with the priest, so that, being changed into the Body and Blood of Christ, which are of the earth and belong to God, it may be a symbol that the whole of reality belongs to God and is blessed with God, then one must, here in this Mass, be resolved to go out into life and do in one's life that which has been done at the altar. One must be resolved to be a courageous fighter, a victor and conqueror; one must be able to say to oneself: "It depends on me; the 'revolution' by which the world is to be converted and return to God must begin with me; I cannot desire and expect the world to grow better, more worthy of God, more full of light, unless that which has begun cosmically and for the whole of history in the sacrifice of Christ now begins uncompromisingly in me too; the thing which I, too, have just been beginning in the sacred rite."

--Karl Rahner, S.J., THE CHRISTIAN COMMITMENT

Further Insights

The Wise King   3 Kings 3 and 4

The name of Solomon is associated with two things: wisdom and royal splendor. Solomon was born and raised like a prince. Having inherited a unified kingdom, he was able to devote his t i m e to administrating its affairs. Toward the end of his life, he asserted his authority by tyrannical methods and fell into idolatry. Investigate: New Testament references to Solomon (Matthew 6:28-29 and 12:42); difference between wisdom and knowledge; "Megiddo" in From the Stone Age to Christianity which gives a description of Solomon's strategic fortress cities.

The Rich King   3 Kings 10

The reign of Solomon was Israel's Golden Age. The Bible gives a long list of the things Solomon did, and the things he had, and infers that under his rule, the king and the people ate, drank and were merry.

The Poor King!   3 Kings 11

But the things he had began to possess Solomon. Indulging every appetite and "enticed by women," the king renowned for his wisdom eventually fell into idolatry and lost the true greatness to which he had been called.

God's Message for Every Mood

When in sorrow
>   Read John 14
When men fail you
>   Read Psalm 26
When you have sinned
>   Read Psalm 50
When you worry
>   Read Matthew 6:19-34
When you are in danger
>   Read Psalm 90
If you have the blues
>   Read Psalm 3
When God seems far away
>   Read Psalm 138
If you are discouraged
>   Read Isaiah 40
If you are lonely or fearful
>   Read Psalm 22
If you feel down and out
>   Read Romans 8:38-39
When you want courage for your task
>   Read Joshua 1
When the world seems bigger than God
>   Read Psalm 89
When you want rest and peace
>   Read Matthew 11:25-30
When leaving home for labor or travel
>   Read Psalms 120; 106:23-31
If you get bitter or critical
>   Read 1 Corinthians 13
If thinking of investments and returns
>   Read Mark 10:17-31
For a great invitation - a great opportunity
>   Read Isaiah 55

Chapter 9 - God Hidden and Revealing

A Freshman Once Said Who are you, God?

"Oh, I know you're the Supreme Being, the Creator of heaven and earth, but that's WHAT you are. I want to know WHO you are. Are you a celestial IBM machine, accurately recording all my good and bad deeds and measuring out 'grace' when I make the proper response? Are you a clever puppeteer, amusing yourself by pulling the strings that make your little earth dolls jump? Are you a harmless old man with a beard, enthroned in an over-stuffed cloud, who must be pacified occasionally by being noticed? Are you, like Santa Claus, the product of someone's imagination? Tell me, God, WHO are you?"

A young man once said to a priest, "I don't believe in God." The priest replied, "Tell me about the God you don't believe in." When the young man had finished, the priest said, "I don't believe in that God either."

1. What did the priest mean by that statement?

2. Why do so many people have mistaken ideas about God?

3. Why is it so important to have a correct notion of God?

Light from the Old Testament

God Reveals Himself...

Wisdom 13:1-9

A child in his father's arms doesn't need a proof of the father's presence. Neither did the biblical man feel any need for rational proofs of God's existence. GOD WAS. He had proved it by His great and gracious deeds and this was all the certainty they desired. This passage from the Book of Wisdom, probably the latest writing of the Old Testament (about 50 B.C.), is a rebuke to those pagans who worship the forces of nature. Having arrived at a sense of the mystery of things, they should have come

101

naturally to a knowledge of God. They are called "vain," that is, stupid for not recognizing God's Hand in the world.

4. If, in his wanderings on the beach, Robinson Crusoe had happened to kick up a pocket watch that was still running before finding his man Friday, would he have had strong evidence that a human being was, or had been, on the island? Why would he never have concluded that the watch "just happened" to be there? Is the universe more complicated than a watch? What would you say about a person who said it came about by chance?

5. St. Francis of Assisi loved his "Brother Sun" and "Sister Water." Have you ever experienced a sense of kinship with the things of nature? Tell the class about it. Give the pros and cons of living in the city, or in the country.

6. Read Father Plunkett's poem, "I See His Blood upon a Rose." Paraphrase one of the verses.

7. Does the workman always put something of himself into his work? What can you learn about God from the things He has made? In what way is "each man's work a portrait of himself"?

Behind all the puzzles, mysteries, sufferings, and difficulties of life there is not a chaos or a jungle; there is the mind and heart of God. The realization that God is a person is the beginning of real religion.
                                        --Reginald McCurdy, WHO IS GOD?

As a Person...   Psalm 17

The God of the Bible, as Pascal noted, is not the God of the philosophers, but the God of Abraham, Isaac, and Jacob. The patriarchs knew Him well. He had bargained with Abraham, wrestled with Jacob, argued with Moses. They had met Him often, not just in the things of nature, but in the events of their lives. To Israel Yahweh was not a thing, a force, a power--He was a living Person. They had experienced His concern for their welfare, His power exercised in their behalf, His demand for their loyalty. They knew Him as one who chooses freely, who gives generously, and who waits patiently.

8. How does a "person" differ from a force or a power? Does a person necessarily have a body?

102

9. Because God is a real person and very close to them, sometimes the biblical writers speak of Him as if He had a body. This is a literary device called an anthropomorphism. Find examples of it in Psalm 17.

10. What is the difference between knowing <u>about</u> a person and <u>knowing</u> a person? How can you get to know a person?

11. Even more important than getting to know a person is getting to <u>be</u> a person. Discuss the effect of the following situations on helping you develop your own personal identity:

   a. Staying close to the gang

   b. Thinking for yourself

   c. Being alone sometimes

   d. Going out of yourself in love to someone else

   e. "Playing a role"

The personal God created man in His image; he, too, is a person. They can communicate only on the condition that both alternately speak and listen, and that both respect the liberty, refusals, and silences of the other. This is the kind of prayer through which we come to "know" God.

Unique...

Isaiah 44

From its earliest history, Israel knew that the God of Abraham, Isaac and Jacob was the only God of Israel. Eventually they came to realize that He is the supreme God, but belief in the existence of other gods for other nations lingered on for centuries. It was the prophets who finally insisted that Yahweh is the God of the whole world, as well as of the Chosen People; that He is not only superior to any other god, but that He alone is God, who created all things, and that all other gods are the handiwork of men.

The supreme message of the Old Testament is contained in the Shema (Deuteronomy 6:4), the Hebrew profession of faith, "The Lord our God is one God!"

12. What other religions today are heirs to the Jewish faith in the one true God?

13. How did this firm belief in one God affect Christ's manner of revealing the Trinity?

Strong...

Psalm 104

When God revealed Himself to the patriarchs, He called Himself "el shaddai," "the Almighty." The words really mean "strong" and "mountain" and form the basis for the trust the people had in their "powerful protector." Their history was filled with His mighty deeds. What He had done with this weak little nation was striking evidence of His power over all nations.

14. The power of God was a source of hope and consolation for the Israelites. Why is it for us so often a source of fear and terror?

And Loving...

Book of Osee

Israel is God's "first-born" because He has chosen it from among all nations to be His special people. Therefore God loves it with a special love and protects it against all its enemies. This love is more than the general concern of the Maker for what He has made; it is the free, personal relationship that entitled every Jew to consider himself a "son of God."

God's willingness to bind Himself to Israel by the covenant is expressed by a Hebrew word "hesed," which means a love that is tender and gracious and steadfast. It is a constant source of amazement that even the repeated faithlessness of Israel does not cancel out the faithfulness of Yahweh. Israel has no doubt that forgiveness is always possible. The wonder is not that God is loving and compassionate, but that His love is so unchanging, so utterly reliable.

15. What is meant by the expression: God loved us into being?

16. To many people the word "love" means many different things. What does it mean to you?

17. Does God's love for individuals differ? In degree? In quality?

The prophet Osee speaks of God's love in terms of a marriage relationship with the details drawn from his own life. Osee married Gomer, but after bearing him three children, she tired of him and took up with other men. Osee was deeply hurt--and angry. When he threatened her, she left him and their children. But he loved her in spite of it and longed to have her back again. Finally Gomer came to her senses and realized how good a man she had rejected. Before he took her back, Osee put her on trial while both looked forward to a complete reunion of love. As he measured God's love for faithless Israel in terms of his own sad experience, Osee gained a profound insight into divine love and patience.

18. What can our experience of loving others teach us about God's love? Can we love God if we have never experienced human love?

Chapter 2 - Osee sees Israel's covenant with Yahweh as a marriage contract, and therefore, in a bold but striking metaphor, he compares Israel's idolatry to adultery. The comparison is especially meaningful because the Chanaanite gods, Baal and Astarte, were regarded as the givers of fertility and were honored by sexual rites contrary to Israelite standards of morality.

19. In what sense did Israel go to her lover Baal for bread, etc.?

20. Where did Yahweh and Israel spend their honeymoon? cf. verse 17.

21. What change of relationship is involved when Israel no longer addresses Yahweh as "baal" (master) but as "my husband"?

22. In what sense can God be said to be a "jealous" God?

23. The metaphor of marital love was destined to grow in other writings of Holy Scripture. Some examples are: Canticle of Canticles; Matthew 9:15; Matthew 22:2; John 3:29; Ephesians 5:25-33; Apocalypse 21:1-4 and 9-10.

24. This marriage symbolism can also be applied to the relationship of the individual soul with God. What details of the ceremony of religious profession are similar to a marriage ceremony?

Chapter 11 - Osee also used the figure of a father's love for his son to explain the mystery of Yahweh's love for Israel. In spite of the authoritarian overtones, the fatherhood of God is portrayed with great tenderness.

25. Compare Osee's description of God's fatherly love with that given by Christ (Matthew 7:9-11).

26. Francis Thompson wrote a beautiful poem of God's love called, "The Hound of Heaven." Find some phrases in it that remind you of Osee.

> Can a mother forget her infant, be without tenderness for the child of her womb? Even should she forget, I will never forget you. See, upon the palms of my hands I have written your name.
>
> Isaiah 49:15-16.

God Conceals Himself...

Exodus 13:21-22
19:16-19
24:15-18

At the beginning of Chapter 33 in the Book of Exodus it says that "the Lord used to speak to Moses face to face," and further on in the same chapter it says, "my face you cannot see, for no man sees me and still lives." This illustrates the mystery of God--He is as close to us as our own being, but at the same time He lives and acts in realms far beyond our comprehension; He is intimate and tender without ceasing to be remote and awe-inspiring;He pours out blessings, but He also sends suffering. In a word, He is both immanent (near) and transcendent (beyond anything material).

...In Mysterious Signs...

3 Kings 8:10-11
19:11-13

In the Old Testament theophanies (appearances of God) God makes His presence known through some natural sign: fire, cloud, thunder and smoke, a gentle breeze, a radiant brightness. Although these signs tell us something of God, they conceal more than they reveal. People who "experience" God have difficulty finding words with which to describe the meeting. Perhaps fire, the most immaterial of all the elements, best shows that a meeting with God is a purifying and transforming experience.

27. What signs did the evangelists use to show the presence of God? Cf. Luke 12:49; Acts 2:3; Matthew 17:1-8.

28. Discuss: Man--every man of whatever century, land, and culture--cannot enter the realm of the spirit except through the door of the senses.

--John Oesterreicher, ISRAEL OF GOD

...In Boundless Immensity...

Psalms 138 and 89

In the course of her history, Israel began to realize the extent of God's power. All things depend on Him, all things are subject to Him--He is responsible for their being. But if He is the Creator of matter, He cannot be a part of it; He is outside matter; He is a spirit. As such He is limited neither by time nor by space. His presence penetrates all things; He is the unfailing source of life whose beginning and end extend into the unknown.Obviously He could not be contained in anything material, so any attempt to make an image of Him was forbidden.

29. Which other religion forbids the use of images? How has this affected the style of their art? Why are Christians not bound by this prohibition?

106

30. How can you determine where a spirit is? Is God present everywhere in the same way, e.g., in your desk, in human beings, in the souls that love Him, in the Holy Eucharist?

31. John is a brilliant mathematician, but he is blind. Jim has 20-20 vision, but his ability in math is practically non-existent. The teacher puts a complicated algebra problem on the chalkboard and explains it. Afterwards both boys say, "Yes, I see the problem." What does each mean? If you had to choose between the two, which kind of sight would you prefer to have? In what sense will you "see" God in heaven?

32. Does the fact of our having a body give us an advantage that God doesn't have? Explain your answer.

33. Because God is a spirit, is it easier or more difficult to communicate with Him?

...In Light Inaccessible

Ezechiel 36:16-31

The unchanging God is completely "other" than the fickle, changing things outside Him. This "otherness" is a mysterious quality--powerful, majestic, frightening, and yet, attractive. Faced with it man is filled with a strong sense of his own nothingness and a profound reverence. This fear of the Lord grows out of the realization of the infinite distance that separates man, even the holiest of men, from the Holy one of Israel.

God's holiness is not merely the absence of all sin; it is positive and absolute perfection, the secret of His being. In this sense only God is holy. Holiness is possible to men insofar as they belong to God. He shares His holiness with those who enter into the covenant with Him. Because they are His people, they, like Him, must love what is good and hate what is evil.

34. Is being holy the same as being very good? Is it the same thing as being pious?

35. In what sense can a "thing" be holy?

36. How did Peter react to the manifestation of Christ's holiness? Cf. Luke 5:8.

37. Americans are notorious for their lack of reverence toward established institutions and customs. Does this in any way affect their attitude toward God?

38. Why is it important to consider both God's nearness and His transcendence in our relationship with God?

Light from the New Testament

The Face of God

John 1:1-18
14:8-11

In the Old Testament God revealed Himself to His people through the events of history as interpreted by the prophets. The revelation was given gradually through many centuries. In the New Testament everything that God is and wants to say to us is expressed in the life and actions of Christ. In Jesus, God speaks His final and eternal Word which resounds forever in heaven and on earth.

In His infinite wisdom God found a way to make Himself comprehensible to men. The Word took flesh and, from His own experience of knowing and loving the Father, was able to interpret the Father for us in words and human gestures. In His humanity men were able to hear, to see, to touch the living God. (1 John 1:1-3)

39. Would you rather have someone you like write you a letter or pay you a visit? Why?

40. Why is a son a good person to tell us what the father is like?

41. In view of God's message to us, why was it appropriate that it should come to us through His son? Cf. John 1:12

The Human Words of God

Luke 15:11-32

In order to reveal to men the mystery of His person and His mission, Christ had to use the ordinary human means of communication--words and actions. Especially by His words He bears witness to His Father and to Himself. In His teaching He explains who He is and why He has come. Very often He uses parables to convey something of His message.

42. What do the following phrases tell you about the father:

  a. "he divided his means"
  b. "while he was yet a long way off, his father saw him"
  c. "ran and fell upon his neck"
  d. "fetch quickly the best robe"
  e. "let us eat and make merry"
  f. "his father came out and began to entreat him"
  g. "all that is mine is thine"
  h. "we were bound to make merry and rejoice"

What did Jesus mean to tell us about God in this parable?

Reward of the Prodigal   Reward of the Elder Brother

PRODIGAL
LEAVES
HOME

NO
RELATION

GENEROUS FATHER
TRIES TO RESTORE ALL
TO HIM

ELDER BROTHER REMAINS AT HOME -
GENEROUS FATHER GIVES HIM GOOD GIFTS EACH DAY

Acts of God Made Visible

St. John tells us that God is Love, but it is as man that He proves it. God gives Himself to us without reserve in Christ. The love of God comes to us through a human heart and is expressed in human acts. Christ's life of "going about doing good" is climaxed by His death on Calvary. In that life and death we have the most convincing testimony of God's love.

43. Can human love be stern? Find an example in the gospel of the sternness of Christ's love; of His tenderness.

So You See...

Our God is an unknown, wonderful God, but He is also an intensely PERSONAL BEING, who calls us to an intimate relation with Himself. Jesus Christ has come out from the heart of the Father to be for us the revelation of the Father. It is through Him that we have access to the family life of the Trinity. He is our Brother who helps us to understand our Father and who gives us His Spirit that we might be good sons as He is.

God is a community of Three who love one another, who depend upon one another. The Father cannot be Father without the Son; the Son cannot be Son without the Father; and the mutual Spirit of love cannot exist without the Two who love. It is to participation in this Community of Love that God has sent His Son to call us.

"The Trinity--the internal glory of God is the Community of People in Love; the external glory of God is the community of people in love." --P. Schoonenberg, GOD'S WORLD IN THE MAKING

44. Why is loving our fellowmen the most important condition for our being admitted to this Community?

45. If nature and revelation and people seem to infer that God is changeable, and even contradictory at times, perhaps it is because our limited vision cannot grasp all He is at once. Compare this situation to what happens when a single ray of light passes through a prism.

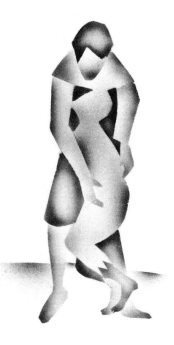

"Every attempt to 'put God into words' will involve a measure of distortion, since we are trying to describe in terms of our own experience someone who is vaster than all our experience." --R.M. Brown, THE BIBLE SPEAKS TO YOU

Glory to God!

Each new realization of who God is should impel us to acknowledge His greatness, to give Him glory. Although our private prayer should always include some genuine expression of reverence and esteem for His Person, it is especially in the liturgy that we give Him the glory that is His due. Christ "introduced into this earthly exile that hymn which is sung throughout all ages in the halls of heaven." (THE LITURGY CONSTITUTION, Paulist Press, 1964) He taught this song of praise to men and we are privileged to sing it with Him. He continues throughout the ages to praise the Father in our humanity, particularly in the Mass and in the Divine Office.

46. Look up the names of the various Hours of the Divine Office and show how they are designed to sanctify the day and night. How do they commemorate the mysteries of our redemption?

47. The prayers of the liturgy, because they express the mind and will of the whole community, are of necessity somewhat formal in tone and general in application, concentrating on the fundamental relationships between God and man. They are usually made from this pattern:

    a. Recognition of God, His supremacy and ability to satisfy our needs.

    b. Recalling of God's willingness to help us as seen from the past.

    c. Expression of need.

    d. Asked with confidence through Jesus Christ our Lord.

Compose a prayer of your own on this pattern.

It's Your Move!

1. How does God reveal Himself in nature?

2. Describe the patriarchs' concept of God? How did they come to this knowledge?

3. Show how the Israelite concept of one God developed.

4. What are the qualities of God's "covenant" love?

5. Discuss the comparison of God's love for His people to marital love.

6. In what does the mystery of God consist?

7. How did the Israelites arrive at the concept of God as a spirit?

8. What is meant by the holiness of God? In what sense can man be holy?

9. Show how Christ is the perfect revelation of the Father.

10. What completely new understanding of God did Christ reveal?

11. What should be our response to the realization of who God is?

Reflection

In Kenneth Grahame's THE WIND IN THE WILLOWS, Rat and Mole were looking for the baby otter who had strayed away, when suddenly they heard the unearthly music of the piper Pan, the god of the animals.

"Then suddenly the Mole felt a great Awe fall upon him, an awe that turned his muscles to water, bowed his head, and rooted his feet to the ground. It was no panic terror--indeed he felt wonderfully at peace and happy--but it was an awe that smote and held him and, without seeing, he knew it could only mean that some august Presence was very, very near."

Mole's wondering glance beheld "the Friend and Helper" and with him, baby otter, safe and content.

"Rat!" he found breath to whisper, shaking. "Are you afraid?" "Afraid?" murmured the Rat, his eyes shining with unutterable love. "Afraid! Of Him? O, never, never! And yet--and yet--O Mole, I am afraid!"

Do you think this aptly describes the Apostles' reaction to the Transfiguration?

Further Insights

A Challenge
3 Kings 18

In one of the most dramatic scenes in all literature, Elias the Thesbite, challenged the power of King Achab, his pagan wife Jezabel, and all the followers of Baal. His heroic faith and courage brought a nation back to the service of the one God.

The following passages tell how a tradition about Elias originated and was finally explained:

4 Kings 2:1-12   Matthew 17:1-13
Malachia 3:23   Matthew 11:11-15
                      John 1:21

Mission Accomplished   John 17

In this beautiful prayer Jesus reveals His relationship to the Father, the message to men with which He was entrusted, and the nature of the response He hoped to receive from them. Can you find these ideas in the prayer?

ALL OF MY LIFE

Sister Germaine, Glenmary Sister

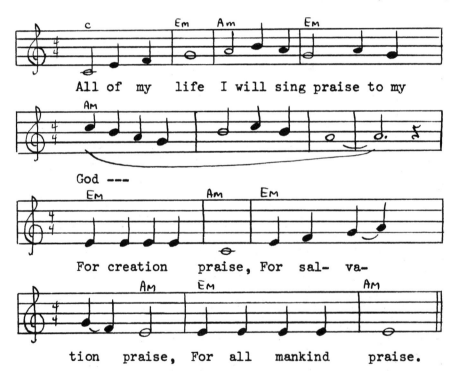

All of my life I will sing praise to my God ---
For creation praise, For sal- va- tion praise, For all mankind praise.

2. To the Virgin praise,
   To the Saints and Angels praise,
   To the Church praise.

3. To the Father praise,
   To the Son sing praise,
   To the Spirit praise.

Chapter 10 -
God's Message Unheeded

A Freshman Once Said
What's so wrong about that?

"People are always telling me, 'Don't do this! Don't do that!' I get tired hearing it. Nobody could keep all those laws. And besides, that would make life awfully dull. It's fun to do forbidden things once in a while. What's so wrong about that?"

1. What is the difference between a sin and a mistake?

2. Could there be sin if there were no laws?

3. What bad effects would follow from sin even if there were no punishment connected with it?

4. Does sin contribute anything to our development as a person? Does it contribute anything positive to society?

Light from the
Old Testament

A Break with
the Brethren . . .

When Solomon's son, Roboam, came to the throne, he listened to wrong advice and declared he would be even more tyrannical than his father had been. The people rebelled and made Jeroboam king of Israel, which was made up of the ten northern tribes. Roboam was left with only Juda and Benjamin in the Kingdom of Juda.

5. What causes division in a family? a school? a nation?

6. Was the division of the kingdom a punishment from God or the natural effect of men's actions?

3 Kings 11:26 - 12:24

In order to keep his subjects from going to Jerusalem, Jeroboam set up sanctuaries at Bethel and Dan, where he placed the statue of the golden calf. These statues were probably to represent the "throne" of Yahweh (ancient peoples often represented their god standing on the back of a young bull), but they soon were confused with the altars of Baal, and many Israelites worshipped at both.

The history of the two kingdoms is a story of disgrace and failure, at least from the point of view of the author of the Books of Kings. He is interested only in how each king kept the covenant, and for most of them he has to report that they "taught Israel to sin." Because the kings were not the models of fidelity to the Covenant that they were supposed to be, God sent the prophets, filled with the fire of His spirit, to enlighten and enkindle the people.

7. *Discuss the relative responsibility of the people who committed idolatry and of Jeroboam, who perhaps never committed the sin himself, but who made it possible for others to do so. Can you think of some modern parallels?*

8. *Prepare a "Meet the Press" program interviewing various individuals for their reaction to the division of the kingdom.*

The Seers

1 Kings 9:3-21 - In every religion there are men who claim to be especially chosen by the deity to make his will known. In the eastern religion they were called "nabi" or "seers." Israel, too, had its seers to whom one went to "consult" Yahweh.

9. *Compare these Israelite seers to the Greek oracles.*

1 Kings 10:5-13 - Out of this natural institution came the professional prophets, bands of men with a strong inclination to religion and great zeal for the things of God. Sometimes they lived around the sanctuaries; sometimes they traveled from place to place preaching and singing the psalms of Yahweh. Their displays of religious fervor often included frenzied chanting and dancing accompanied by flutes, cymbals and bells.

Among them were false prophets, willing to say anything they thought would please a client, especially if the client would greet the good news with a generous tip. (Micheah 3:5) However, most of them were honest and dedicated and did much to preserve devotion to Yahweh, when devotion to Baal seemed more profitable.

10. *A true prophet has to be willing to say things people don't want to hear. What does that tell you about the life of a prophet?*

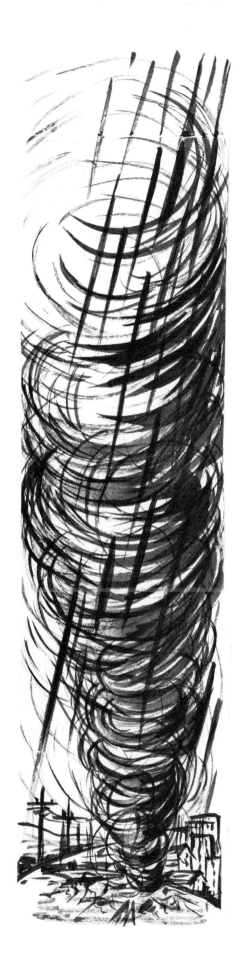

Called by God

But the most noble and influential representatives of the prophetic office were the <u>vocational</u> prophets. Each was favored at the beginning of his career with a soul-shaking religious experience that left him a changed man.

<u>Amos 7:10-16</u> - Amos was a shepherd from Tekoa, a short distance from Bethlehem, whom Yahweh "took" from his flock and sent to Israel with a warning. What this "taking" involved, we shall never know, but it left Amos with the firm conviction that he had a mission and that God truly spoke by his mouth.

11. Do you know of any other occasion on which people were "taken" by God? There is a very interesting account in THE CROSS AND THE SWITCHBLADE of a young minister, Reverend David Wilkerson, who was "taken" by God from his comfortable parish in Philipsburg, Pennsylvania, to work with teen-age gangs in the jungles of New York City.

<u>Isaiah 6:1-13</u> - The youthful Isaiah received his prophetic calling while at worship in the Temple. The liturgy he was performing suddenly gave way to the Reality it stood for and Isaiah was confronted with the all-holy God. The vision of God's holiness filled him with dismay at the sinfulness of His people, until he realized that God's most ardent wish is to share His holiness with His people. Isaiah responded to God's invitation with all the zeal of his generous and courageous nature.

12. Which two prayers of the Mass are taken from this account?

13. Most people do not consider it a compliment to be called "holy." Is this due to a

wrong idea of what is meant by holiness or to a distaste for the things of God?

Jeremiah 1:4-19 - Jeremiah lived at a turning point in his people's history. He presided over the passion and death of his people and their burial in Babylon. He foretold their resurrection and the institution of a new covenant. But he needed much persuasion and the assurance of God's unfailing support before he accepted the mission of delivering God's final message, "Repent or perish!"

14. Which words of God to Jeremiah are echoed in Christ's words to His apostles in Luke 12:11-12?

Jeremiah 20:1-18 - Jeremiah suffered greatly for delivering God's message; he was scourged, imprisoned, publicly denounced. He was often tempted to ignore his commission to speak, but his "sense of God" was too strong for him.

15. Have you ever been in a situation in which your conscience required you to say things that would make you unpopular? What positions often put people in that predicament? What can be done to make it easier?

Ezechiel 1:1-3:15 - Ezechiel's vision of God is very much in keeping with his sensitive, highly imaginative personality. The four living creatures who bore the throne of the Almighty represented the best in creation: man--intelligence, ox--strength, lion--majesty, and the eagle-- speed. The wheels represent God's omnipresence and the eyes, His wisdom. This is surely the transcendent God, and Ezechiel is a mere mortal, a "son of man." The first duty of his painful task was to convince the people that their hopes for the safety of Jerusalem (Ezechiel had been taken to Babylon with a group of political hostages before the fall of the city) and for a quick return there were vain. He resorted to significant pantomimes performed in public to attract attention and arouse discussion.

16. Ezechiel's vision is a challenging subject for the arts. Many artists have attempted to portray it. Why don't you give it a try?

17. The four living creatures have become well-known symbols in the Church. What do they represent?

18. The Cherubim are Yahweh's throne-bearers. Compare the way we picture the superior nature of these members of Yahweh's court with the Hebrew representation. Which do you prefer?

Israel's Conscience

The prophets were men of their times, vitally concerned with national and international affairs. But they saw these events with the eyes of God, and men were not always happy with what they saw. As their name implies, their mission was to "speak in behalf of," not to "foretell." It was their mission to touch men's hearts so that they would "return to the spirit which Yahweh had breathed into Israel in its creation." They stood up fearlessly among their fellowmen and proclaimed with supreme confidence "Thus says the Lord...."

"I Hate Your Feasts!"

<u>Amos 5:21-27</u> - What God really wants is a man's heart. He cannot bear the empty signs of worship they offer Him.

<u>Isaiah 1:10-20</u> - Isaiah lashed out at the hypocrisy of external religious practices that do not spring from a heart that loves God.

19. Compare the thought of these passages with that of Matthew 5:23-24.

20. If Isaiah or Amos came into your parish church some Sunday morning, what might he have to say on this same topic?

"My People Have Deserted Me!"

<u>Isaiah 46</u> - The prophets jeer at the idols, the helpless things for which the Israelites have abandoned the Almighty One.

<u>Jeremiah 2</u> - Through His prophet God speaks like a jilted lover, stung to the quick by the beloved's preference for what is obviously less good.

21. Discuss: We no longer worship idols, but sometimes we put "strange gods" before the true God.

"The Cry of the Oppressed Accuses You!"

Amos 5:7-17 - Petty thievery, unjust prices, conniving judges, greedy merchants--all come under the ban of the prophet.

Micheah 2- The oppression of the poor by the rich is a crime calling to heaven for vengeance,and the prophet threatens punishment to Judah.

22. *Which recent encyclicals confirm the prophets' teaching in this respect?*

Amos 4:1-3 and 6:4-7; Isaiah 3:16-26 - The prophets lash out at the national leaders and the haughty women, who tolerated and encouraged dishonest practices. They do not condemn wealth as such, but merely the injustice and oppression of the poor which so often accompanies it.

23. *What modern practices would the prophets condemn? What civic movements would they get behind and push?*

"You Rely on a Broken Reed!"

Isaiah 31 - When the kings, in order to defend their tiny country, wanted to make alliances with the great powers, the prophets protested that Yahweh was their protector, that political treaties were a poor substitute for the covenant.

Isaiah 7 - When Isaiah tried to persuade Achaz to put his trust in Yahweh instead of in Assyria, he promised that the advancing enemies would be turned back, and that God would give the king a sign of His fidelity. Achaz pretended to be shocked, but Isaiah told him of the mysterious child, Emmanuel ("God with us"),who would be a sign of God's presence among His people. Unfortunately, Achaz preferred to sacrifice his own son to the god Moloch, rather than to depend on Yahweh's unusual sign, which was partially fulfilled in Achaz' son, Ezechiah.

24. *How does St. Matthew (1:22-23) interpret this passage? Holy Scripture sometimes has a more profound meaning that is apparent only after the prophecy has been fulfilled. Isaiah could never have imagined in what a wonderful way God would be "with them."*

25. *Is it "practical" to trust God?*

Breathing Threats . . .

Amos 5:18-20 - Those who wait so expectantly for the "Day of the Lord," when He will finally overcome all His enemies, should beware lest on that day they find themselves to be the object of His wrath,instead of sharing in His triumph.

Jeremiah 19:1 - 20:6 and 13:15-19 - The smashing of the potter's flask was a dramatic attempt to make the Israelites realize the fate that was in store for them. But the threatened destruction could still be averted; God's dealings with men to a great extent depend on men.

26. *Discuss: Punishment is not the same as revenge; it can be motivated by love.*

> *That there was a deluge once seems not as great a miracle as that there is not one always.*
>
> SIR THOMAS BROWNE

27. *Before you go to confession the next time reflect on this passage from Jeremiah 3:11-25.*

Jeremiah 7:1-15 - The people of Juda had come to regard the Temple as a kind of good luck charm. Nothing could happen to Jerusalem or to them because the House of Yahweh was indestructible. Jeremiah's thankless task was to warn them that God would not hesitate to destroy even the Temple if they did not change their ways.

28. *Which words of Jeremiah have practically the same meaning as those of Christ in Matthew 7:21?*

29. *Could Catholics make the same mistake that the people of Judah made? What might they regard as their guarantee of salvation?*

...and Promises

Isaiah 11:1-10 and 9:1-6 - Isaiah foresaw that Juda would be destroyed, that the royal tree of David would be cut down, leaving only the roots and the stump. But he knew, too, that God's promise would not fail, that the Israel of faith would survive and so he spoke of a new shoot that would sprout from the stump--a future king of David's family who would be powerful and good, and would bring peace.

30. *What do the references to the animals in the passage mean? To what extent has this prophecy come true?*

119

31. Where have you heard verse 2 before? What meaning does it have in this passage?

32. Examine the Advent and Christmas Masses in your missal for texts from Isaiah. Which passages are used most frequently? Why is the Book of Isaiah sometimes called the "pre-Christian" gospel?

33. Write a paraphrase of the O-antiphon from the Divine Office (December 19) that is based on this passage.

Amos 9:8-15 - Although many of the Chosen People failed to keep the Covenant, there were, in every age, a small group of faithful who bore witness to God's fidelity to His promise. Having been purified by suffering they form the nucleus of the Kingdom. This "remnant" would return from exile and rebuild Jerusalem.

34. The Church is built on the "remnant." Discuss this idea in connection with these texts: Matthew 7:13-14 and 20:16.

Jeremiah 31 - Although God allowed Israel as a nation to die, He did not desert His people. He promised that He would make a NEW covenant with them which would never be broken. Its law would be written, not on tables of stone, but on men's hearts. The bond that united God and His people would be much more personal. Reward and punishment would depend to a much greater extent on the individual and less on the nation.

35. To what extent do you suffer from the wrongdoing of other members of your family? school? Church? Is this unjust?

The Light Goes Out!

4 Kings 17 - In 722 B.C. after a three-year siege, Sargon II, king of Assyria, conquered Israel, the northern kingdom, and deported the cream of the population (27,290 according to his records). Then they brought in foreigners who eventually intermarried with the wretched Israelites who had been left behind. These people were the Samaritans, whom the Jews despised for their "half-breed" ancestry. Thus Israel lost its identity as a nation and became known as the "ten lost tribes of Israel."

36. Read the account of Our Lord's conversation with the Samaritan woman (John 4:4-26) for evidence of the disagreement between the two groups. What special meaning does the Parable of the Good Samaritan have against this background?

Jeremiah 52 - The day foretold by the prophets finally came in 587 B.C. when Nabuchodonosor's army broke through the walls of Jerusalem, burned the city and the temple, and deported thousands into Babylon.

37. *Read Psalm 136, the sorrowful expression of a homesick people.*

Ezechiel 34 - When Jerusalem had fallen to the Babylonian army and the people who survived were taken into Babylonia, a dark cloud settled over the exiles. They were shocked and sobered by what at first seemed like abandonment by God. Then Ezechiel changed his tune and painted bright pictures of the future. He condemned the negligence of the former shepherds of Israel, their kings, and assured them that Yahweh Himself would take charge of the flock. He would send another David to be the perfect shepherd of His people.

38. *Read John 10:1-18 to meet the promised Good Shepherd. See how Jesus takes an Old Testament theme and draws new conclusions from it. In gratitude, read Psalm 22.*

Light from the New Testament

The Great Prophet

Jesus is considered not merely as a prophet of the New Testament, He is THE Prophet. He can claim this title on two counts: 1. All prophecies are fulfilled in Him; and 2. He announced the beginning of the New Era, the establishment of God's Kingdom on earth.

39. *Here is some evidence that Christ considered Himself a prophet: Luke 4:23-24 and 13:33; and that others considered Him one: Luke 24:19 and Matthew 21:11.*

But He was a prophet in more than name and reputation. His whole life and work were carried out in the spirit of the prophets.

Witness to Truth

John 7:25-53

The mission of the prophet is a difficult one because men do not always want to hear the truth. Sometimes they would rather settle for half-truths or for what seems to be, instead of for what really is. The playwright T.S. Eliot, in his MURDER IN THE CATHEDRAL, has Archbishop Thomas Becket say "human kind cannot bear very much reality." Prophets invariably provoke controversy and dissension.

40. How can we discover truth in the midst of confusion and falsity?

41. People who do not want to hear the truth will try to get rid of prophets. Discuss the various means that are often used:

    a. Try to change or CORRUPT him; make him conform to crowd standards.

    b. Try to SILENCE him; use ridicule, scorn, or isolation.

    c. KILL him, if all other means fail.

    Show how these methods were used against Christ.

42. Every Christian is called to be a prophet for his times, to bear witness to truth. Discuss: We must be willing to pay the price which the truth requires of us.

Religion of the Heart
Matthew 21:12-13 and 23

Prophets are people whose <u>sense of God</u> is so powerful that they can always see the DIVINE DIMENSION in the HUMAN SITUATION. The central truth of his message is always that INTERNAL COMMITMENT IS MORE ESSENTIAL THAN EXTERNAL OBSERVANCE. And some Jews did not want to hear it, anymore than you would want to hear that you have failed a test.

43. If Christ were to give this sermon some Sunday in your Church, what examples might He use to show how we make the external observance more essential than the internal commitment?

44. When a Doctor of the Law at another time asked Christ what He thought was the most essential thing in religion, what did He answer? Cf. Matthew 22:34-40.

45. Write a paper on one of the following topics:

   a. The Prophets in My Life (that is, those who witness the truth for you).

   b. The Prophets--Men of Faith (They saw the world with the eyes of God.)

   c. The Prophets--Men of Their Times (They were the conscience of their people.)

   d. A Prophet Looks at America in the Twentieth Century (Would they see the same things as they saw in their day?)

So You See...

We can never really understand "what is so bad" about the wrong things we do, until we come to some understanding of God's greatness. This was the mission of the prophets--to bring home to God's people a realization of His majesty and His love and an awareness of what it means to take a stand against Him. Each of the prophets cast some new light on the mystery of man's rejection of God.

The Holy One of Israel

Isaiah raised Israel's understanding of God to a new level by his repeated emphasis on divine holiness. In God, holiness is not merely moral goodness; it is the divine Self-hood (so completely different from man) which enters into all His relations with His creatures. Each of His works is the expression of His holiness. His work of creation, His work of salvation, His covenant works are mighty and gracious deeds because He is Power and Goodness. So what He is (His holiness) shines forth in what He does; it cannot be otherwise. Man's "holiness' is never more than a poor imitation of God's.

46. Cardinal Newman once said: "It would be better for the sun and moon to drop from heaven, for the earth to fail, and for all the millions who are upon it to die of starvation in extreme agony, as far as temporal affliction goes, than that one soul, I will not say should be lost, but should commit one single venial sin." Why is it difficult for us to accept this statement?

47. The saints often spoke of their sinfulness in what seems to us an exaggerated way. How could they have been sincere in what they said?

But because he is associated so intimately with God, man must, as far as he is able, share His ideals and standards of action. Because God is Justice, and Truth, and Mercy, man must strive to be just and honest and kind. God says: "For I, the Lord, am your God, and you shall make and keep yourselves holy, because I am holy." (Leviticus 11:44)

48. The Israelites were the first of the ancient peoples to connect morality with religion. What is the difference between the two? What does this tell you about the difference between false gods and the One True God?

49. God made a pact of friendship with us without any real merit on our part. The only proper response for us is the effort to "live up" to this privilege. The French expression "noblesse oblige" describes our situation very well. What does it mean? How does it apply to us?

50. Someone once said that the phrase "noblesse oblige" means that nobility is defined by its obligations rather than by its privileges. Do you agree or disagree? Why? Name a few persons who have shown real nobility. Are their privileges a sufficient reward for the burden of their duties? What do you consider the most satisfying reward for the exercise of responsibility?

JESUS ANSWERS A LAWYER'S QUESTION: "Thou shalt love the Lord thy God with thy whole heart, and with thy whole soul, and with thy whole mind. This is the greatest and the first commandment. And the second is like it, Thou shalt love thy neighbor as thyself. On these two commandments depend the whole law and the Prophets." Matthew 22:37-39

The Shell of Sin

Only gradually did the Israelites come to understand the true nature of the response that God expected of them. Early in their history this consisted mainly in the observance of religious rites. Sin was the failure to carry out exactly these rites that set them apart from the nations. The sin was always something exterior, and sometimes the "sinner" was not even aware that he had done anything wrong.

51. Show how the idea of sin in these passages is very incomplete:

   a. 1 Kings 14:24-46   b. 2 Kings 6:6-8

The prophet Amos in his violent complaints against the emptiness of worship suggests that sin is not merely a bad act. When we see sin only as the breaking of a law, or as the legal penalty incurred for not fulfilling an obligation, we are guilty of legalism.

52. Dave was out with a crowd of fellows after a basketball game on Friday, when someone suggested that they have a hamburger. It seemed like a good idea to Dave and he thought to himself: "I might as well. I can go to confession tomorrow." Show how Dave's idea of sin is incomplete.

53. Bonnie stayed home from Mass last Sunday because she had a heavy cold. When she went to confession the next time, she confessed missing Mass "just to be sure." Why is Bonnie's idea of sin incomplete?

54. Jesus condemned the Pharisees for their legalism. Read John 18:28 and 19:31 for examples of their great concern for external observances. What basic principle of morality were they violating at the same time?

The Heart of Sin

It was the prophet Osee who taught that sin is not merely an injustice, a breaking of the law, but that it is an act of ingratitude, an infidelity, a rejection of God's friendship.

55. Andy and Jack were very close friends until Jack started going with a gang who broke into houses "just for kicks." Jack said he still wanted to be friends with Andy, but he wasn't willing to give up his new pastime. Why can't their friendship continue under these circumstances? If Jack continues to go on his "little expeditions," is it equivalent to rejecting Andy's friendship? How does this resemble our relationship with God?

56. Ordinarily the Bible talks about "sin," not "sins." In other words, no matter how many different kinds of bad actions there are, there is only one sin at the root of them all. What is the common denominator of all sins? Does this give you a clue as to why no serious sin can be forgiven unless the person is sorry for all his serious sins?

Because our friendship with God is not perfect, we need laws to help us know what is pleasing to God and to re-enforce our love when it falters. But friendship for God may ask more things of us than the law requires.

57. What might God ask you to do as a friend that is not required of you by any commandment?

58. When John has to clean up the school grounds as a detention assignment, he does as little as possible. But when he does the same kind of work for old Mr. Woods, of whom he is very fond, he often works overtime and is always looking for new ways to make the yard attractive. Why the difference? How does this apply to our dealings with God?

The Community Bloodsucker

The ancient Semites had a strong sense of the solidarity of the family and the nation. If a member of the clan were injured, the whole clan was injured and sought to take revenge on the offender's clan for the injury. In like manner they expected the sin of the individual to be visited upon the whole family or nation. (Cf. Numbers 16:25-34) Ezechiel had to remind them that the individual is judged on his own merits. (Ezechiel 18:1-32.)

Gradually the truth emerged. Although each person is responsible for his own salvation, yet salvation can be achieved only within the community. Therefore, although the individual is responsible for his sin, yet sin is not merely a <u>private</u> affair. Every sin weakens the bond that unites the community to God and lowers the level of its spiritual life. Every offense against God is also an offense against our brothers.

59. *How can sin hurt God? Ourselves? Our fellowmen?*

60. *The Jackson boy who lives next door to Dave got into trouble with the police. Dave noticed that the whole Jackson family stayed indoors and began to avoid their friends and neighbors. Even the six-year old twins played alone in their backyard. Why did they react this way? Should the sins of our fellow Christians affect us this way?*

If you content yourself with confessing your sins without struggling against sin in yourself and in the world in which you live, you will never overcome evil. If you content yourself with struggling against the evil in yourself and in the world in which you live without confessing your sins, you will never win your struggle.

--M. Quoist, THE MEANING OF SUCCESS

The Signs of Conversion

If, as St. Augustine says, sin is "aversio a Deo et conversio ad creaturam," then conversion is a retracing of one's steps, a turning back to God. And just as the inner decision to be independent of God is expressed by the sinful action, so the repentant sinner looks for some exterior sign to show his inner "change of heart."

The liturgy provides occasions by which the Christian can acknowledge that he has been unfaithful both to God and to his brothers.

a. On Ash Wednesday we wear blessed ashes on our forehead. All year we confess our sins privately, but at the beginning of Lent we publicly proclaim that we are sinners and we desire to atone for our misdeeds during the coming season of penance.

61. *Report to the class on the ceremony used by the early Church to begin the season of public penance. (Cf. C. Howell, OF SACRAMENTS AND SACRIFICE.)*

b. The first prayer said in common by the celebrant and the people at the Holy Sacrifice of the Mass is a nine-fold plea for mercy. We cannot reaffirm our covenant with God without first recognizing the harm our sins have done to our own souls and to our brothers in Christ.

62. *What does the prayer of the Pharisee and that of the Publican (Luke 18:9-14) tell you about their ideas of sin?*

c. God forgives our sins as soon as we are truly repentant, and He immediately renews the bond of friendship. The Sacrament of Penance, however, gives us an opportunity to express the repentance that we feel and to receive the sensible assurance of God's forgiveness. It is also the means by which we are reconciled to the community of God's people, from whom we have separated ourselves by our sin, and to be given again the right to partake in the Community Meal, which we had forfeited.

63. *If God forgives our sins as soon as we are truly sorry, why must we, if we have committed a serious sin, go to confession before receiving Holy Communion?*

64. *Why can't God forgive sins until we repent of them?*

"Would you refuse a gift because you didn't like the person who delivered it? What difference does it make who the priest is who hears your confession, for he holds in his hands the fruits of the death and resurrection of Jesus Christ."
—M. Quoist, THE MEANING OF SUCCESS

I have loved thee with an everlasting love.

JEREMIAH 31:3

Bible Vigil in Preparation for the Sacrament of Penance

(The general format is the same as that on pages 25-27. Make these substitutions.)

ENTRANCE HYMN: Lord Have Mercy (Kyrie) from a familiar Mass

FIRST READING: Ezechiel 18:20-32

(Commentary) The prophet reminds us that it is not enough merely to recognize our wrongdoing and to recite it accurately to the priest. The essential condition for obtaining forgiveness is the "turning away" from our sins, the turning to God with a "new heart and a new spirit." It implies a sincere desire to give up sin and to live for God.

RESPONSE (ALL): We confess to almighty God,
    to Jesus Christ, our spokesman and savior,
    to Mary, the holy mother of God,
    to all the saints in heaven,
    and to all here present,
that we have sinned
    by our thoughts,
    by our words,
    and by our deeds.
Therefore we ask Jesus, our spokesman,
    Mary, the holy Mother of God,
    all the saints in heaven,
    and all here present,
    to pray to the Lord our God for us.
May almighty God have mercy on us,
    forgive us our sins,
    and bring us to life everlasting.
May the almighty and merciful Lord
    grant us pardon, absolution
    and remission of our sins
    through Jesus Christ. Amen

--Rev. Theodore Stone, A DAY OF RENEWAL.

SECOND READING: Ezechiel 34:11-16

(Commentary) Long before Christ applied the name to Himself, the prophets had likened God's vigilance and solicitude for His people to that of the shepherd devoted to the care of his flock. He does not wait for the strays to find their way back--He goes to seek them. He does not scold and berate them for their waywardness--He binds up their wounds and feeds them. This is the God we meet in the Sacrament of Penance.

128

RESPONSE

LEADER: I myself will look after and tend my sheep.

ALL: The Lord is my shepherd; I shall not want

LEADER: Beside restful waters he leads me; he refreshes my soul.

ALL: The Lord is my shepherd; I shall not want.

LEADER: He guides me in right paths for his name's sake.

ALL: The Lord is my shepherd; I shall not want.

LEADER: Even though I walk in the dark valley I fear no evil.

ALL: The Lord is my shepherd; I shall not want.

LEADER: For you are at my side with your rod and your staff that give me courage.

ALL: The Lord is my shepherd; I shall not want.

LEADER: Only goodness and kindness follow me all the days of my life.

ALL: The Lord is my shepherd; I shall not want.

LEADER: And I shall dwell in the House of the Lord for years to come.

ALL: The Lord is my shepherd; I shall not want.

THIRD READING: Isaiah 53: 2-12

(Commentary) The suffering that Christ was willing to undergo for our sake helps us to realize the extent of God's love for us, and the firm basis for trust in committing ourselves to Him. He can want nothing for us but what is for our good. Every confession should bring us closer to that complete surrender to God and the abandonment of all that is not God.

RESPONSE

LEADER: As obedient children, do not conform to the lusts of former days when you were ignorant;but as the One who called you is holy, be you also holy in all your behavior; for it is written, "You shall be holy, because I am holy."

ALL: Into your hands I commend my spirit; you will redeem me, O Lord, O faithful God.

LEADER: What does the Lord, your God, ask of you but to fear the Lord, your God, and follow his ways exactly,to love and serve the Lord, your God, with all your heart and all your soul, to keep the commandments and statutes of the Lord which I enjoin on you today for your own good?

ALL: Into your hands I commend my spirit; you will redeem me, O Lord, O faithful God.

LEADER: Can a mother forget her infant, be without tenderness for the child of her womb? Even should she forget, I will never forget you. See, upon the palms of my hands I have written your name.

ALL: Into your hands I commend my spirit; you will redeem me, O Lord, O faithful God.

LEADER: I will get up and go to my father, and will say to him, Father, I have sinned against heaven and before Thee. I am no longer worthy to be called Thy son.

ALL: Into your hands I commend my spirit; you will redeem me, O Lord, O faithful God.

LEADER: Forgetting what is behind, I strain forward to what is before, I press on towards the goal, to the prize of God's heavenly call in Christ Jesus.

ALL: Into your hands I commend my spirit; you will redeem me, O Lord, O faithful God.

RECESSIONAL HYMN: Lamb of God (Agnus Dei) from a familiar Mass.

Further Insights   *The Elephant and the Mouse*

Isaiah 36 and 37

The Assyrians are known as the Nazis of the ancient world. Their efficient war machine left their victims no choice but surrender or destruction. When Sennacherib laid siege to Jerusalem, Isaiah counseled resistance and promised that Jerusalem would not be taken. The retreat of the Assyrian host, which is recorded even by the Greek historian Herodotus, is generally attributed to an attack of bubonic plague. But whatever the cause, mighty Assyria bowed before tiny Juda like Goliath before David, who trusted in the Lord.

Accept this Yoke !

In the face of the Babylonian threat, Jeremiah warned the people: "Do not resist! Babylon is unknowingly God's punishing rod. Submit humbly to this purifying trial." As a constant reminder to the people that revolt would end in slavery, he appeared in public with a wooden yoke around his neck. The people called him a defeatist, a pacifist. Anania, a false prophet, openly contradicted his position and defiantly broke the yoke he wore. Jeremiah predicted that the broken yoke would be replaced by one of iron.

Dry Bones

Israel in exile is like a field of dry bones. The chosen people had lost the Spirit of Yahweh and could do nothing unless He chose to bring them back to life. But Ezechiel assured them that God had not abandoned His people.

65. Write a paragraph interpreting Ezechiel's vision as the resurrection of the sinner from the death of sin.

The Song of the Vineyard

Isaia 5:1-7 - This is a masterpiece of Hebrew lyrical poetry and we can almost hear the prophet's lyre accompanying the song. The vineyard was a favorite theme for love songs in the Old Testament.

66. The vineyard seems to have been one of Our Lord's favorite
themes, too. See how He uses it in the following parables:

Matthew 20:1-16   Luke 13:6-9
Matthew 21:33-41   John 15:1-8

67. Polly's elder sister Pat is an accomplished dancer. While
she was performing in the school play, her heel caught in
the hem of her skirt and she literally "fell on her face" in
front of the whole student body. Sister Alice was trying to
console her after the embarrassing incident and said that
the Lord was "dunging" His fig tree. What did she mean by
that expression?

It's Your Move!

1. What caused the division of the Kingdom?

2. According to what standard did the biblical writer judge the kings of Judah and Israel? What was his verdict?

3. Describe the purpose and activities of the professional prophets mentioned in the Bible.

4. What was involved in the call to be a prophet?

5. In general, what was the mission of the prophets?

6. Of what four sins did the prophets accuse Israel?

7. What arguments did the prophets use to persuade the people to repent?

8. How successful were the prophets?

9. Show how all the elements of prophecy are present in Our Lord's life.

10. Why is it so difficult for us to realize the malice of sin?

11. What are some ideas of sin that are incomplete?

12. What is the essence of sin?

13. Why is sin not merely a private affair?

14. What is involved in repentance?

15. What are the special benefits of the Sacrament of Penance?

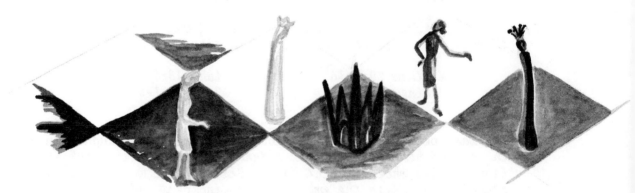

+

FEAR NOT

Brother Val Habjan, S.M.

Fear not, O fear not, fear not for you have more value than

spar - rows, ma-ny spar - rows, spar - rows that your Fa- ther

formed in His Hand. formed in His Hand.

1. I have seen you shiv- er in the cold, trem-ble in the wind

a - lone. But ...

2. I have heard you fleeing in the night,
   Hiding from a fear unknown.

3. I have heard your tears in the rain
   Washing on my heart of stone.

4. I have known your gentle call,
   Winging from a nest that's bare.

5. I have seen your Maker smile,
   Watching all the while you play.

6. I can be that sparrow,
   Trembling in the wind,
   Fleeing in the night,
   Nesting in the heart of God.

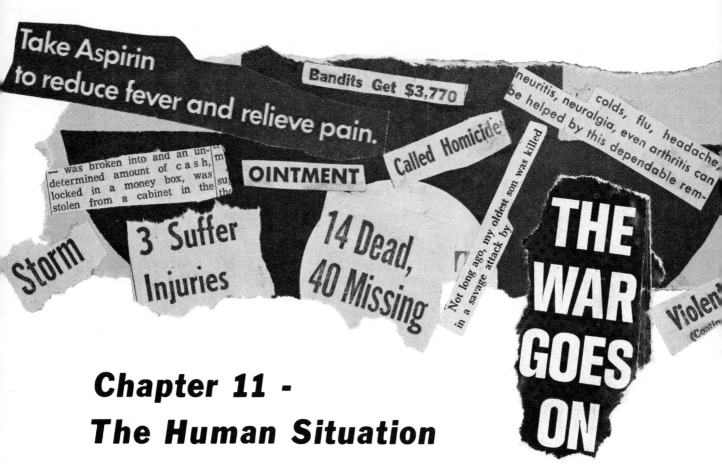

Chapter 11 -
The Human Situation

A Freshman Once Said
Why so many aspirins?

"Drugstores must sell millions of them every year. Headaches, tooth-aches, arthritis, cancer--why is there so much pain in the world? Then there are fires, floods, accidents, death--why so much suffering? Besides that, the cheaters win, honest people get robbed, liars succeed, hard work-ers lose their jobs--why so much injustice? If I loved someone, as you say God loves us, I wouldn't let these things happen if I could stop them. Can't He stop them, or doesn't He care enough?"

1. What difference is there between knowing something will hap-pen and causing it to happen? Can you know that something is going to happen and at the same time not want it to happen? Give an example.

2. Are we ourselves the cause of some of the suffering? Give some examples.

3. What good can come from suffering?

Light from the Old Testament
Why, Lord?

Jeremiah 11:18-12:4

For many centuries Israel's faith in the goodness and justice of God took for granted that the good would have a long and prosperous life and the wicked would meet failure and an early death. Their knowledge of the after-life was limited to belief in a shadowy existence in Sheol, the land

Pain

Four-year-old refugee, belly swollen by malnutrition, puts away chicken and noodles from a can of C-rations.

Big Blizzard Made Plains 'Stand Still'

Killed In Jet Crash

TABLETS

Nervous, swollen,

Heart Attack Fatal

Officer Robbed During Probe

minor cuts and scratches

Innocent Pleas

Man, Woman Die In Traffic Here

Fall Against Bus, Pillar Crash Fatal

The shocking statistics of driving accidents

COUGH SYRUP

of the dead. Since it did not include a system of rewards and punishment, God's accounts had to be balanced in this world. When the people of Juda were taken into exile in Babylonia, some of them complained that God was punishing them for the sins of their ancestors. "The fathers have eaten green grapes, thus their children's teeth are on edge." (Ezechiel 18:2)

The prophet's answer, which emphasized the responsibility of the individual, gave them something to think about. As long as they thought in terms of the whole people, it was true that the good prospered and the wicked did not. But when they began to think in terms of individuals, they had to admit that sometimes the wicked prospered and the innocent suffered. They could not help asking with Jeremiah, "Why, Lord?"

4. *What answer to this question do you have that had not yet been revealed to these people?*

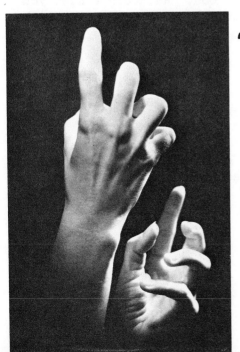

The Impatience of Job

The Book of Job is one of the outcomes of this thinking. The unknown author uses a popular prose story about "a blameless and upright man from the Land of Hus" as the prologue of his work. A lively dialogue between Job and his consoling (?) friends on the theme of how a just God can permit an innocent man to suffer forms the body of this poetic and psychological drama from Israel's wisdom literature. The "patient" Job gives forth a torrent of complaints that will pierce even the highest heaven.

The Prologue - Chapters 1 and 2 - T h i s is the proverbial Job, blessing God in the midst of his afflictions. The sons of God are heavenly beings who 135 surround the Lord's throne; Satan, "the adversary," is one of them. The name has not yet come to mean the enemy of God and man. The Prologue sets the stage for the rest of the play--Job, impoverished and covered with boils, surrounded by his sympathetic friends.

5. Which part of the Mass for the Twenty-first Sunday after Pentecost is taken from the book of Job? Why is this verse so appropriate for this part of the Mass?

6. Which passage from the Prologue is a beautiful prayer for times of sorrow?

7. Discuss Satan's statement that anybody can be good as long as things go well, that the real test of a person's worth is how he reacts in time of suffering or misfortune.

If the conversation between Job and his friends were reduced to bare essentials, it would be something like this:

Chapter

3:1-6	Job:	"I wish I were dead! My troubles are so great."
4:1-9 and 5:6-8	Eliphaz:	"Only the wicked are afflicted; therefore, confess your wrong-doing and God will show you mercy."
6:24-30	Job:	"Tell me what I have done wrong. Is it possible that I cannot see my own sins?"
8:1-7 and 20-22	Baldad:	"If you were really innocent, we would know it by the favors God would shower on you."
10:1-7	Job:	"God, you see that I am innocent. Why do you treat me as if I were guilty?"
11:1-6 and 13-16	Sophar:	"Just listen to him! He claims to be innocent although the sign of God's judgment is clearly on him."
13:1-10 and 15-19	Job:	"I was speaking to God. He doesn't need you to defend Him with your lies. He can speak for Himself."
18:5-21	Baldad:	"He has already spoken in the misfortunes which always come to the wicked."
21:7-17	Job:	"I know some wicked people who live very comfortably."
22:2-11	Eliphaz:	"You must have done some of these evil things, or at least omitted the good ones."
31:2-37	Job:	"If I had done those things, I would have nothing to say. Let God be my Judge!"

38:1-30 and 40:1-14 Yahweh: "If you will answer my questions, I will answer yours. Who am I? And who are you?"

42:1-6 Job: "You are the Sovereign Lord—and I am your creature. So be it."

8. *What solution does the author give to the problem of the suffering of the innocent? Does this seem to put a gulf between God and man? How was this gulf bridged?*

9. *The powerful and imaginative descriptions of nature in Yahweh's speech are strong and beautiful poetry. Choose one that appeals to you and memorize it. The passage on the horse is one of the most famous. For the Hebrews, the horse was a really decisive weapon of war, something like our atom bomb.*

<u>The Epilogue, 42:7-17</u> - God praised Job, rebuked his friends, and then displayed His Providence by restoring Job to his former position.

10. *Father Ellis, in THE MEN AND THE MESSAGE OF THE OLD TESTAMENT, summarizes the judgment on Job and on his friends in this way: "For Job, God is more mysterious, but He is more God. For the friends, God is less mysterious and correspondingly less God."*

11. *Some critics think the drama was weakened when the author had God restore Job to his former position. What do you think?*

12. *Job's problem still plagues people. Archibald Macleish in his Broadway play "J.B." presented the dilemma in modern terms. His solution puts the spotlight not on God, but on man, and tends to idealize man in his suffering. Prepare a report for the class on Macleish's play.*

The Servant Songs
Second-Isaiah

A century after the death of Isaiah an anonymous writer addressed the humbled and discouraged exiles in Babylon in some of the most beautiful and inspiring poetry of the Old Testament. The opening verses, "Comfort, give comfort to my people," give the theme of his writing, which is called THE BOOK OF CONSOLATION and comprises chapters 40 and 55 of the Book of Isaiah. Israel had paid the price for its sins and deliverance was at hand in the person of the Persian general Cyrus. The prophet assured them that God had not rejected them; they were still His People entrusted with the mission of making Him known to the world.

A key figure in the mission was the mysterious "Servant of Yahweh" described in four short poems. It is difficult to say to whom this title refers, whether to the "remnant" of Israel who have remained faithful in all their sufferings or to an individual person who ideally represents the faithful "remnant."

13. A beautiful example of the poetry of Second-Isaiah is 49:14-18. If you ever doubt that God loves you, read this reassuring passage.

42:1-4 - Yahweh's trusted servant with His help will bring holiness to all nations.

14. Which details of this passage are also in Mark 1:9-13?

15. Today the word "servant" implies a humiliating position. But if you think of it in terms of "one who renders service," you discover many "servants" in very honorable positions. Name some of them.

16. What is the Lord's attitude toward His servant?

49:1-6 - In spite of seeming failure, Yahweh's servant will not only restore Israel, he will bring salvation to the world.

17. What references to this passage do you find in Matthew 15:24-28 and Luke 2:32?

50:4-11 - The servant speaks of how the Lord supported him in his suffering. He tells of the security of those who walk in the darkness of the Lord and the fate of those who make their own light.

18. Notice the similarity between this passage and Matthew 26:67.

52:13 - 53:12 - For centuries the Israelites had been sending the scapegoat out into the desert, burdened by their sins, to die in their place. In this passage the servant voluntarily assumes this role, to die that others might be released from their sins and live. He will achieve his glorious mission by the distasteful way of suffering and death. Because this idea was so contrary to the expectation of the King Messiah, they were never associated in the popular mind.

19. The servant suffers because he is faithful. What suffering will fidelity to God bring into your life?

20. Sometimes we must lose a battle in order to win the war. Have you ever won a victory by being defeated?

21. When would you expect these songs to be used in the liturgy? Check your missal to find some examples.

22. This is not a pretty picture of the Messiah. Should artists' representations of Him be pretty? Explain.

Judaism--The Fruit of Suffering   Ezechiel 36:22-36

In the dark soil of the exile there grew a new understanding of Israel's mission. Her destined glory lay in becoming not a world empire, but a worshipping community. Henceforth, any form of idolatry was unthink-

138

able. The Kingdom of Israel had been transformed into the Faith of Judaism which would rest on two pillars.

The Temple

1 Esdras 1 and 3

The Persian king Cyrus, who conquered Babylonia, was a capable and energetic ruler. The prophets hailed him as "Yahweh's Anointed" because of his decree allowing the Israelites to return to their land and to rebuild the Temple. The obstacles were many--shortage of labor and material, opposition from the snubbed Samaritans and the ever-present threat of discouragement--but the devotion of Joshua and Zorobabel, the crown-prince of Juda, never flagged in the 20-year project. The solemn dedication of the second temple took place amid the laments of the older people who remembered the glory of the first.

23. The Bible quotes (1 Esdras 6) the official records of the Persian Empire, which show a surprising consideration for the religious beliefs and practices of the tiny country under their control. How do you account for this attitude?

24. In the Second Book of Esdras we meet Nehemiah, whose efficiency and drive sparked the efforts to rebuild Jerusalem. From the material in chapters 1 to 6 prepare a report on this dauntless leader, whom we can't help but admire.

The Law

From the bitter experience of their past, the Jews realized that they would find it difficult to preserve purity of worship. They abandoned all hope of political independence and adopted the Torah (the Law of Moses) as the constitution of the Jewish commonwealth. The local government was put into the hands of the priests and their assistants, the levites, and under their supervision, the Law was applied to every aspect of their lives civil, social and personal.

These people were a nation apart with a unique mission. Special practices, like not eating everything the pagans ate, the strict regulation of marital relations, circumcision and the observance of the Sabbath, were a protection against pagan contacts. This "Wall of Law" tended to isolate the Jews from their neighbors and eventually led to narrow-mindedness, but in this age it was most necessary that they have the support which the Law gave them.

25. The people of God have been referred to as "Hebrews" and "Israelites," but this is the first time they have been called "Jews." What is the significance of this?

26. What religious practices have you found helpful in preserving and strengthening your relationship with God? What dangers should you be aware of in carrying out these practices?

27. Dave's cousin Peter was dating a Jewish girl, but her family was so opposed to it that he finally broke up with her. Pete told Dave that he thought that Catholics were the only ones opposed to mixed marriages. Explain the situation to him.

28. Using Nehemiah's words, "with one of his hands he did the work and with the other he held a sword" (2 Esdras 4:17), as the theme, write a description of the Christian's progress through life.

29. Many typically Jewish institutions originated during this period. Look up the following words in the Catholic Biblical Encyclopedia (New Testament) or in the Encyclopedic Dictionary of the Bible and give a report to the class: Amen, Law, Mishna, Scribe, Synagogue, Sanhedrin, Levite, Gentile.

Light from the New Testament

Memo to Job

Just discovered a new angle to your recent inquiry about the suffering of the just man. Read in Second-Isaiah about an innocent individual who volunteered to share in the sufferings of his guilty people so that he could bring them with him to a happier life. Noticed, too, that many good people suffered the Babylonian Captivity and that their suffering made it possible to begin life again in the New Israel. Doesn't solve the mystery, but I thought you might like to work on these clues.

30. Women suffer much in bearing a child. Why do they do it so willingly?

"Thy Holy Servant Jesus"   Acts 4:30

Israel had always gloried in the title "Servant of Yahweh;" it was an honorable title. And when Jesus came He, too, made it clear that He had come to be of service.

Matthew 12:15-21 - His heart overflowed with compassion for the people and He did what He could to relieve their misery. At the same time He tried to avoid irritating the Pharisees unnecessarily.

141

<u>Mark 10:35-45</u> - His desire to be of service is so great that He is willing to give His life that "many" may be freed.

<u>John 13:1-15</u> - Jesus acts out His servant role with love and humility in order to inspire His followers to imitate Him.

31. *Read Luke 1:38 to meet another "servant" of the Lord.*

"By His Stripes..."   Isaiah 53

When Jesus wanted to tell the people that He was the Promised One of God, He did not call Himself the Son of David, the Royal Messiah. Instead He chose two obscure titles from the Old Testament, the glorious Son of Man and the Suffering Servant. He combined these as if to say that He would achieve His mission and come to glory through the unlikely way of defeat and suffering.

<u>Luke 18:31-34</u> - Since the Apostles knew no Messiah except the Messiah King, they could not understand when Jesus spoke of His passion and death.

<u>Psalm 21</u> - Because the evangelists quote the opening verse of this psalm as Our Lord's prayer on the cross, we conclude that the whole psalm is an expression of His sentiments as He lay dying.

32. *Which other phrases besides the opening verse suggest the circumstances of His death? What is the spirit of the last ten verses?*

<u>Acts 8:26-35</u> - The early Church used the Servant theme to proclaim the central truth of Christianity, that salvation consists in being associated with Christ in His passage from death to life.

33. *Up until the time of His passion and death did Jesus live a rather ordinary life? Did He suffer more than most men? In His passion and death did He suffer more than the two thieves crucified with Him? Did He ever give the impression that it is a good thing to suffer? What gave His suffering more value?*

"...We Are Healed"

Pain of itself has no power to help others, but pain borne out of love can bring peace and healing—it is redemptive.

<u>John 11:47-54</u> - Caiphas unknowingly speaks a great truth: this one man's death would mean life for all the people.

<u>Romans 5:5-11</u> - Because God loves us, Jesus became one of us and involved Himself in the suffering and death that is the lot of men. His acceptance of this human condition with its painful burdens is evidence of

142

the power of His love. It is this power that destroys sin and death and enables man to begin a new life of love of God and of His fellowman.

1 Peter 2:18-25 - Because we had lost our power to go to God, God came to us, and the coming involved the cross. A love that reconciles is a love that costs, and Christ was willing to pay the price. And we who have been bought with that love must strive to love our fellows in the same way.

34. Examine the gospels for evidence of Christ's attitude toward suffering. List your findings in two columns: 1. Courage in the face of personal suffering; and 2. Compassion for the suffering of others.

"With His bleeding hand, Christ cancelled our debt; with His crucified body, He crossed out our misdeeds; with a love never seen before. He turned the load of guilt into a lever of grace.
          --J. Oesterreicher, THE ISRAEL OF GOD.

So You See...

People have been asking the question you asked for many centuries. There have been partial answers, but no one has been able to give a completely satisfying explanation of why a good God permits so much suffering in His world. Let us look at the evidence.

Common Sense Says...

Some suffering is our fault. The world we live in necessarily has some fixed laws as to how things work. We cannot expect God to suspend these laws when for some reason or other they work against us. For instance, if you get in the way of a fast ball, you shouldn't expect not to have at least a lump and a headache. Or if your favorite indoor sport is cutting people down to size, you can't blame God if you're not very popular.

35. Bring to class from the news media some examples of suffering for which people are responsible and some which cannot be traced to human causes.

Suffering is not good in itself; in most cases, it is evil and should be eliminated. However, it can have some good effects.

36. Show that Christ during His lifetime and the Church ever since have worked to eliminate suffering. To the elimination of what suffering that exists today should Christians be dedicated?

37. What is your reaction to persons who have never developed the qualities of sympathy and compassion? What are the root meanings of these words?

Job Says...

Some suffering is punishment for sin, but it is the discipline of a loving Father who is concerned about the habits and personal development of His children. When it's a case of innocent people suffering, there isn't any answer except for those who have actually experienced God's goodness. These know that He can never be anything but good in spite of seeming evidence to the contrary. This trust in God's integrity was later justified by a new understanding of an after-life in which the good are rewarded and the wicked punished.

38. Communists accuse Christians of depending so much on the justice of the next world that they are not concerned about righting wrongs in this world. Do you think that religion is the "opium of the people"?

Jesus Says...

Suffering and death are the normal conditions of human living. No one escapes them. To prove that God is not insensitive to your plight, I have come to share it with you and to show you how love can transform your suffering into a creative force in the world. Just as My willingness to suffer what you suffer releases the life of God into the world, so your loving acceptance of whatever is painful in your life can increase that flow of divine life in yourself and others. I will not take away your suffering, but I will give it meaning and purpose and thus make it bearable.

39. WILLIAM C. was all set to start his pre-med training when his father died and he had to give up his plans and go to work. Bill is hurt and bewildered and a little bitter as he asks over and over again, "Why did this happen to me?" What would you tell him?

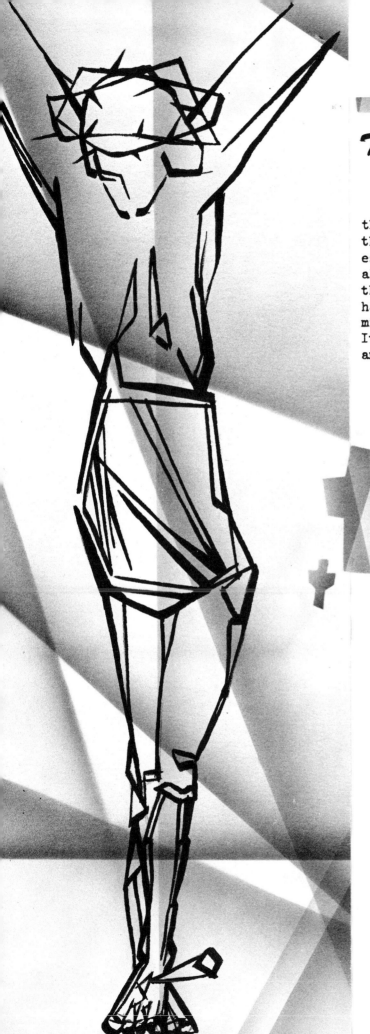

The Sign of the Christian

Galatians 6:14-15

Ever since the time of Constantine the best known sign of Christianity is the cross. It is everywhere--on churches, on sacred vessels and vestments, in all the ceremonies. This does not mean that Christians are morbid. To one who has faith, the cross is an eloquent reminder of how much God cares about us. It is also the sign of Christ's victory and His entrance into glory.

40. At different periods in our history the cross has expressed different aspects of the mystery of our redemption. W h a t ideas are expressed by: a plain wooden cross? a cross set with precious jewels? a crucifix depicting Christ naked and bleeding? a crucifix depicting Christ in royal robes or priestly vestments?

41. Make a large cross with the corpus made up of a mosaic of illustrations of the suffering members of Christ's Body with an appropriate saying o r title.

42. Plan a classroom ceremony to venerate the cross. Cf. Service for Good Friday and Mass of the Exaltation of the Cross, September 14.

43. Discuss t h e Catholic practice of making the Sign of the Cross and what it should mean to us. Cf. SACRED SIGNS, Romano Guardini, p. 13-14.

145

Suffering with Christ

The Church has a special sacrament for the suffering Christian. When illness weakens the body and makes it difficult to pray, through the Sacrament of the Anointing of the Sick the Christian is united to the suffering Christ and thereby enabled to make his personal suffering redemptive. This sacrament also helps him to face the final suffering of life in union with his Savior and supported by His dispositions.

44. The Sacrament of the Anointing of the Sick is a means by which physical suffering can be consecrated. How can you consecrate ordinary aches and pains and the mental suffering of everyday living?

It's Your Move!

1. Why did the Israelites think that prosperity equaled goodness and that suffering equaled badness?

2. What helped them to realize that this is not always true?

3. What is the problem of the Book of Job?

4. What solution does the author give to the problem?

5. What is the theme of the "Servant Songs" from Second-Isaiah?

6. Show how these songs can refer to the faithful "remnant" of Israel?

7. What new understanding was the fruit of Israel's suffering in exile?

8. Why was it so important to the Jews returning from exile that the Temple be rebuilt?

9. Why did the Law assume such great importance during this period?

10. What effect did this emphasis on the Law have on the Jewish people that is still evident today?

11. Why did Christ choose to be known as the Son of Man rather than as the Son of David?

12. In what sense is Jesus the Suffering Servant of Yahweh?

13. What does common sense tell us about suffering?

14. What did Jesus do instead of telling us why there is suffering?

15. How can you make suffering bearable?

16. What does the cross mean to a Christian?

17. How can suffering become a redemptive force in the world?

Reflection

A PRAYER FOR MERCY AND FORGIVENESS

I

Out of the depths
I have cried to thee, O Lord:
Lord,
hear my voice.
Let thy ears be attentive
to the voice of my supplication.

II

If thou, O Lord, wilt mark iniquities:
Lord, who shall stand it?
For with thee
there is merciful forgiveness:
and by reason of thy law,
I have waited for thee, O Lord.

III

My soul hath relied on his word:
My soul hath hoped in the Lord.

IV

From the morning watch
even until night,
Let Israel hope in the Lord.
Because with the Lord
there is mercy:
and with him
plentiful redemption.

And he shall redeem
Israel
from all his iniquities.

--Psalm 129

Chapter 12 -
God's Masterpiece Defaced

A Freshman Once Said

Is the world worth saving?

"When I read about all the murders and robberies and dope addiction that go on, even among other kids, I begin to wonder. And then I turn the page and it's gang wars and race riots, graft in high places and double-dealing everywhere. I get very discouraged and wonder why God bothers with a world like this. Maybe a great big atom bomb is the answer."

1. Not so long ago there was a popular song called "The Eve of Destruction" which expressed very similar ideas. Do you agree with them? Give your reasons.

2. If this is the situation, should Christians withdraw as much as possible from contact with the world so as not to become contaminated?

3. Would you say that since Christ died to save the world, His work to a great extent has been in vain?

Light from the Old Testament

Actually the question that has been posed is a very old one. In fact, the author of the Book of Genesis wrote the first eleven chapters to answer it.

In the Beginning

Genesis is part of the Torah, the five books of the Bible which contain the teaching of Moses. During the exile, when the Old Testament books of the Bible as we know them today began to take shape, three accounts of the ancient traditions of the Israelites were combined and edited in the Book of Genesis. Its first eleven chapters form a kind of prologue to the Bible.

The history of Israel, which began officially with God's revelation of Himself to Abraham, was a dialogue with God. Israel had met Him in repeated historical events. He had given this insignificant group of ordinary men a goal and a purpose for living, but their traditions told them nothing about what He had done before He chose them for His people. So in the light of their experience,and under the inspiration of the Holy Spirit, they gave an account of His relations with man in the hundreds of thousands of years that we call pre-history.

Because they knew Him as the only God, they concluded that all things that are depend on Him. They knew Him too as a saving God and saw creation as the prelude to all His saving acts. These great religious truths are the heart of the message of Genesis 1 to 11.

4. *What other writings are named for their opening words?*

God Builds a Palace ...
Genesis 1:1-2:3

How to present these profound truths posed a problem because the authors had no information about the people or the times. They were familiar, however, with the stories that the Babylonians, the Assyrians and the Egyptians told about the origin of the world and its inhabitants. They would write a similar story that would outshine all the legends of the pagan gods because it contained the truth.

5. *What similarities do you find between the Genesis account of creation and this Babylonian account written about 2000 B.C. ? Marduk, the city-god of Babylon, defeated the she-monster Tiamet, the symbol of chaos, and constructed the universe out of her carcass. One half formed the solid earth, the other half became the firmament which holds back the upper waters. Then he made and installed the sun, moon, and stars. Finally he created mankind by mixing the blood of a rebellious god with clay so that men could serve the gods and supply them with nourishment.*

Both accounts of creation are based on the very limited knowledge of the universe gained from observation. To these people the earth seemed like a platter-like formation covered by a huge bowl (the firmament). They knew there must be water above the bowl because sometimes it leaked through in rain and snow. The rivers and seas were evidence that the platter was floating on water. The sun, moon and stars marched across the firmament like an army and were called "the hosts of heaven." Light was a separate element since it was often present when the heavenly bodies were

not, for example, on cloudy days. The heavens were a three-storied affair
with the birds occupying the first level, the heavenly bodies the second,
and high above the upper waters, "in excelsis," God dwelt in the third
story.

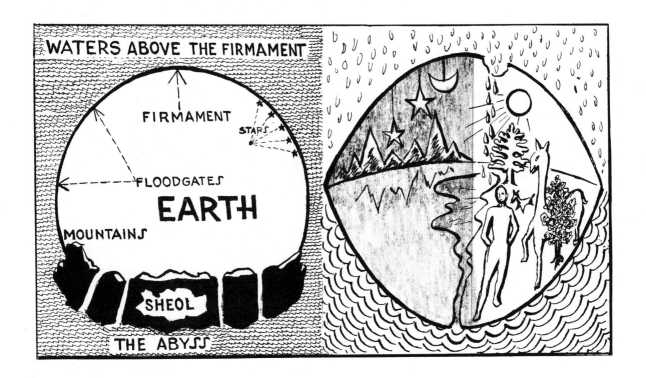

The World of Genesis

6. Using the above illustration, show how in the creation ac-
    count God is a very orderly workman, first building the
    structure and then furnishing it. Notice also that He is a
    good Jew because He keeps the sabbath.

Although the author of Genesis uses the same vivid imagery and the
same primitive science as the pagan stories, he makes a point of correct-
ing their false notions of God.

7. How does the author of Genesis show that he does not accept
    these pagan ideas:

    a. The sun, moon, stars, even animals and trees are gods.

    b. The gods and the world both came from uncreated world
        matter.

    c. The world is an accident, the by-product of a war between
        angry gods.

d.   Material things are the evil handiwork of an evil god.

8.   Prepare a report for the class on Father Pierre Teilhard de Chardin, the world famous paleontologist (a fossil expert). Even as a child, he was fascinated by the mineral world and searched for secrets in stones and stars. All God's creatures spoke to him of their Creator and, like Francis of Assisi, he could relate to them in a very wonderful way.

9.   Why can't the account of Genesis be of any help to scientists who are trying to discover how the world originated? Is the Scripture account an argument against evolution?

10. The Russian cosmonaut returned from his trip in space with the report: "I saw no God through the portal of my craft." Astronaut Cooper, aboard his capsule "Faith 7" on his seventeenth orbit around the world, was moved to say: "I thank you, Lord, for all these startling, wonderful things that You have created." How do you react when you look at the wonders of nature, whether in the great outdoors or in the lab under the microscope?

11. Collect pictures that illustrate the beautiful things God has made. Project them on a screen as the class prays Psalm 103.

...For the King of Creation

Genesis 2:4-17

Genesis has two accounts of the creation of man and both of them emphasize the great dignity that is man's because he is made to the image of God. The first account (1:26-27) says he is like God because he is the lord of the earth and all things in it, just as God is the Sovereign Lord of the universe. The second account also tells of man's special gifts but does so by the use of vivid symbols:

    a wonderful garden - to a desert people, an ideal situation
    the tree of life - like a fountain of youth -- immortality
    the tree of knowledge of good and evil - the right to determine what
        is right and wrong (God retained this right for Himself).

12. Compare Marduk's process of making man with that of the author of the second Genesis account.

13. Robert McAfee Brown (THE BIBLE SPEAKS TO YOU) illustrates the difference between factual and poetic writing by revising Shakespeare's famous words from AS YOU LIKE IT (II, i, lines 16-17): "...tongues in trees, books in the running brooks, sermons in stone," to read "trunks in trees, stones in running brooks, sermons in books." Both versions convey truth. Compare their effectiveness.

14. What great powers do we have because we are made to God's

image? Why did God give us these powers?

15. *Does this likeness of man to God depend on the color of his skin or the degree of his intelligence? Upon what does it depend? What does the Declaration of Independence attribute to this fact?*

16. *How is our natural likeness to God raised to a new level? Cf. Romans 8:29 and 2 Corinthians 3:18. How is it defaced?*

17. *The gift of life is a never-failing source of inspiration to all forms of art. Arrange for the class to see or hear some of these works glorifying the creative power of God through the creative power of men working in various media:*

In sound - the oratorio THE CREATION by Joseph Haydn

In color - the Sistine Chapel ceiling by Michelangelo

In stone - the sculpture THE HAND OF GOD by August Rodin

In movement - the ballet LA CREATION DU MONDE by Darius Milhaud

18. *The special love and forethought of God in creation are simply expressed in this excerpt from James Weldon Johnson's "The Creation," from GOD'S TROMBONES:*

...Then God sat down
On the side of a hill where He could think:
By a deep, wide river He sat down;
With His head in His hands,
God thought and thought,
Till He thought, "I'll make me a man!"
Up from the bed of the river
God scooped the clay;
And by the bank of the river
He kneeled Him down....
This Great God,
Like a mother bending over her baby,
Kneeled down in the dust
Toiling over a lump of clay
Till He shaped it in His own image;
Then into it He blew the breath of life,
And man became a living soul.
Amen. Amen.

The whole poem captures, in the spirit of another day and another culture, the rhythm and phrasing of the biblical account.

... And the Queen

In a society where might made right a woman had no rights. The pagans believed that it was a man's world because nature had ordered it so. But the sacred writer outlined the role of woman in God's plan. She was:

"like Adam" - made to the image and likeness of God

"a helper" - supplying something he was lacking

And both were:

"two become one flesh" - forming a community of love

"unashamedly naked" - loving the person, not merely the body

"fruitful" - sharing God's creative power

19. List the ways in which men and women complement each other, that is, each supplies what is lacking in the other.

20. What makes sex different in man and in animals?

21. Take time out to think about your own sense of dignity. Praise God in the words of Psalm 8.

Seeds of Revolt

Having testified to the goodness of God and of all the things He made, the sacred writer now has to account for the evil that flourishes in the world. He says that man's taste of godlikeness made him thirst for complete independence, that his desire to be a law unto himself is the cause of all sin, and that from the root of sin springs all the evil in the world. The story of Adam and Eve is really the story of Everyman and Everywoman in which each of us sees himself.

"the serpent said" - evil personified in the hated Chanaanite snake-god

"you will be like God" - you will be completely independent

"she took of its fruit"- she acted, rejecting God's standard and deciding for herself.

22. Every temptation follows the same pattern as Eve's. Do you recognize the various steps of the process?

a. You question the rightness of God's command.

153

b. You concentrate on the arguments in favor of the sinful act.

c. Sin becomes very attractive.

d. Desire for it becomes very strong.

e. A choice is made.

Identify the various stages in the biblical account.

23. Dramatize the conversation that goes on between the devil and a teenager he is tempting. Cf. SCREWTAPE LETTERS, C. S. Lewis.

24. The experience of temptation is no disgrace; it merely testifies to the fact that we are human. Using these Scripture texts, write a paragraph on the Christian's attitude toward temptation.

a. 1 Peter 5:8
b. 1 Corinthians 10:13

c. Luke 22:40
d. James 1:12

The Bitter Fruit

Genesis 3:7-24

The picture that the author paints of man after his sin is uncomfortably familiar. It makes us realize how much we resemble our first parents. The effects of sin are drastic and far-reaching.

"they realized that they were naked"	- man lost his inner harmony and experienced the rebellion of his lower appetites
"they hid themselves from the Lord God"	- man lost his intimacy with God; he no longer "knew" Him
"the woman you placed at my side"	-men turned against one another
"enmity. . .between your seed and her seed"	- man will have to fight against evil
"he shall crush your head"	- evil will be overcome
"distress in child-bearing... In the sweat of your brow... unto dust you shall return."	- pain difficulties death are inevitable in a society in which violence and selfishness have replaced the order of reason
"placed the Cherubim...to guard the way"	- man lost forever the favorable situation intended for him

25. The expressions "tree of life" and "cherubim" were in common use among the ancient peoples of the Near East. Prepare a report for the class on their meaning. Cf. Encyclopedic Dictionary of the Bible or Catholic Biblical Encyclopedia. Report to the class on the Greeks' explanation of evil in the story of "Pandora's Box."

26. The second (Yahwist) account in Genesis uses many anthropomorphic expressions in describing God's activity. Note the irony with which God speaks in Genesis 3:22. What does He mean?

Original sin is more than just the first human decision to reject God's standards which had certain legal consequences on the whole race of men. Original sin is an atmosphere in society, a frame of mind, a scale of values, which is no longer God-centered. It is in the air we breathe, the traditions we inherit. Who of us has not experienced that strong but secret repugnance for what we recognize to be good, that shamefaced but real affection for what we know to be evil? Even the most innocent of us cannot approach God with a clear conscience, infected as we are with the virus of sin. And how shall we be inoculated against its sinister effects?

27. Read Psalm 50:7 and Romans 7:18-19 slowly, trying to share the psalmist's and St. Paul's sense of sin. Then ask to be delivered from it in the words of Psalm 50:12-14.

The Abundant Harvest

Genesis 4 - 11

The sacred writer here illustrates how the contagion of sin spread. When man stepped out of his proper relationship with God, he was at odds with his whole environment.

4:1-16 - Cain and Abel were sons of Adam in the same sense that we are. The names and the setting of the story are both Hebrew. The murder of the shepherd lad by his farmer brother paints a vivid picture of how sin sowed hate in the hearts where only love should grow.

28. Considering the history of the Israelites why do you think the shepherd was the "good guy" and the farmer the "villain" of the story?

29. One of the Christmas seals from Father Flanagan's Boy's Town pictured a young boy carrying a sleeping child on his back. The caption read, "He ain't heavy, Father...he's m' brother." Compare this lad's attitude to Cain's.

6:5 - 9:17 - There are many ancient records of a great flood. The story was told and retold and the sacred writer used parts of two versions, not very neatly joined, to tell how God hates sin and punishes wickedness, but also how He takes care of those who serve Him faithfully.

30. Read the Mesopotamian account of the flood as told to Gilgamesh by Utnapishtim (LIGHT FROM THE ANCIENT PAST, Jack Finnegan, pp. 35-6). Report to the class any similarities you find to the account in Genesis.

31. *If we are conscious of our sinfulness, we must be still more conscious of God's fidelity. The unchanging bounty of nature (8:22) is the visible reminder of the constant will of God to give gifts to man. Pray Psalm 66.*

32. *Why is the ark a symbol of the Church?*

<u>11:1-9</u> - This last story in the Prologue to the drama of redemption is a Babylonian folk legend explaining the origin of languages, but the biblical writer uses it to show that men cannot create unity among themselves without God. There is no communication, no real understanding without love, and we cannot genuinely love our fellowmen except in God.

33. *In what sense is Pentecost (Acts 2:3-12) the reversal of Babel?*

34. *When ambition drives us to "make a name for ourselves," and to leave God out of the planning, let us pray Psalm 126:1-2.*

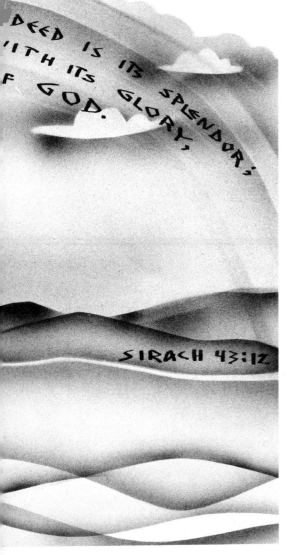

DEED IS ITS SPLENDOR, WITH ITS GLORY, F GOD.

SIRACH 43:12

With the Prologue ended, the stage was set for the opening scene of the history of salvation. The glorious plan of creation was shattered. The noble creature, who was to have been God's vice-regent, was caught in a mesh from which he could not escape. But God was watching and waiting. In His own good time He would come to free man and to piece together the scattered fragments of His plan in a mosaic more marvelous than the original.

35. *Why do you think that Genesis 3:15 is sometimes called the First Gospel?*

36. *Why can the sin of Adam and Eve in the Easter Vigil Service be called a "felix culpa," a happy fault?*

37. *Since the fall, man has a dual personality, capable both of noble deeds and of foulest crimes. This is a favorite theme of literature. Tell the class about a movie or a book in which the main character exhibits this dualism. For example, there is Captain Ahab, a "grand ungodly god-like man," in MOBY DICK; and there is the famous DR. JEKYLL AND MR. HYDE. You might even know some real-life characters who qualify.*

Light from the New Testament

A New Beginning

John 1:1 - 18

Like Genesis John's Gospel has a prologue. It is so like the opening chapter of the Bible that we cannot escape the conclusion that John is making a connection between the two events. Once again God speaks His eternal Word and there are "light" and "life" and "a living being." But this time His word is not merely the power of God entering into matter and transforming it.It is God Himself entering into flesh that He might become "what we have heard, what we have seen with our eyes, what we have looked upon and our hands have handled."(1 John 1:1) His love found a way to overcome man's dullness of heart and vision by becoming one of them and sharing their laughter and pain, their joys and sorrows, their hopes and fears.

38. How does St. Luke's account of the Incarnation (1:35-38) resemble the Genesis account of creation (1:2)?

A New Adam

Philippians 2:5 - 11

When God became man He entered fully into the human situation. His Godhead, suspended (so to speak) for a while--St. Paul says He "emptied Himself"--He had no resources to call upon other than those available to every human being. He had to work and suffer and pray and finally, die, like every other man. He asked for no exemptions.

39. The humanity of Christ stands out most clearly in the Gospel according to Mark. Read these passages slowly trying to realize how perfectly human His reactions were in the ordinary circumstances of life:

3:5	8:2-3	8:11-12	10:21
4:38	5:43	9:35	12:37b

You can find examples in the other gospels also.

There is only one thing in which He was unique--He was not like the rest of men, estranged from His Father or from His brothers. He came from God with divine love welling up in His heart, never having learned to prefer Himself to others. And no matter what men did to Him, He continued to love His Father who had sent Him and the men to whom He had been sent. By His perfect fidelity to love, He earned the right for His human nature to be filled with divine glory and to share His power to love and the glory that radiated from it with the brothers to whom He was so devoted.

40. The love of Christ for His Father and for us finds its most touching expression in the Gospel according to John. Read these passages slowly trying to enter into the spirit that filled Christ:

14:31   8:29   13:1   17:24-26

A New Creation

When Christ rose from the dead, He was not restored merely to life on a natural level. He was filled with the Life of the Spirit, and on the very same day He began to pour out that Spirit into the hearts of His followers. They, too, would give this Life-giving Spirit to others, and Christ would continue to be incarnate in men's flesh until the end of time.

The strangle-hold of sin was broken. In Christ man has access to the transforming Spirit that can bring about a new MAN, a new HEAVEN, and a new EARTH.

41. Study the diagram and from it show how God's fidelity is greater than man's sin.

The Saving Acts of God

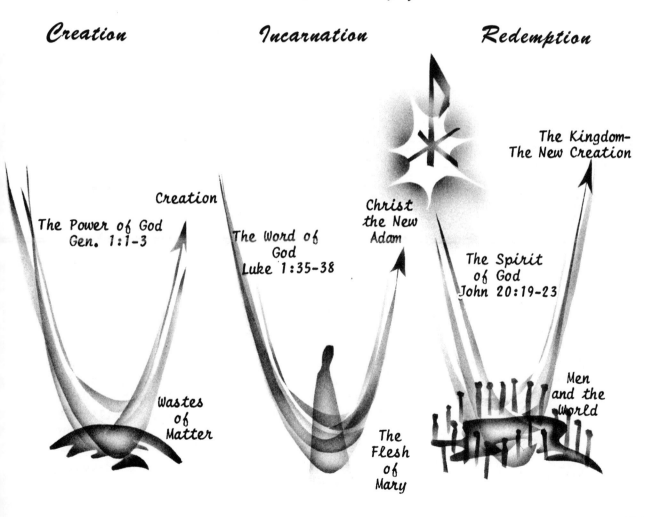

Creation   Incarnation   Redemption

The Power of God
Gen. 1:1-3

Creation

Wastes
of
Matter

The Word of
God
Luke 1:35-38

Christ
the New
Adam

The Flesh
of
Mary

The Kingdom-
The New Creation

The Spirit
of God
John 20:19-23

Men
and the
World

159

So You See...

It's a wonderful world God made--but still incomplete. Each generation discovers new marvels, but there remain immense reaches of space to be explored, rich stores of minerals to be discovered, intriguing secrets of the atom to be revealed. God put the responsibility for bringing the world to fulfillment into the hands of men. He said to Adam. "Fill the earth and subdue it!" But the disorder, confusion, and chaos which flowed from man's sin had its effect also on the world of matter, and it, like man, needs to be redeemed.

Man is redeemed by the Incarnation of Christ and the infusion of His Spirit. Matter, too, can be transformed by the action of a life-giving spirit.

pile of stones	+	design	=	cathedral
eleven men	+	team spirit	=	86 - 0
words	+	idea	=	poem
ingredients	+	recipe	=	cake
two persons	+	love	=	new life

42. *What transformations take place when spirit and matter come together in the examples above?*

The World Awaits You!

Romans 8:14 - 22

We, who have received the Spirit of Christ in baptism, have a special obligation to help redeem the world. Each according to his own abilities must continue Adam's struggle to re-order the forces of the world, to do what he can to make our world a home for man, where each one can develop all his human qualities.

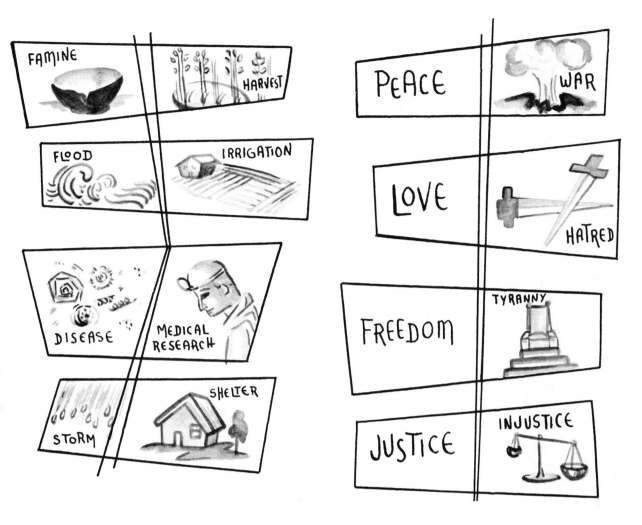

43. Name a person or a group of people who have played a role in bettering our world. Find one example for each illustration. Show by references to the gospel how these works are a continuation of Christ's work in the world. How do they help to bring God's design to fulfillment?

"When Christians put themselves to work, even if it be in a task of a temporal order, in conscious union with the Divine Redeemer, every effort becomes a continuation of the effort of Jesus Christ and is penetrated with redemptive power. It thus becomes a more exalted labor, one which contributes to a man's spiritual perfection, and helps to impart to others on all sides, the fruits of Christian redemption." --Pope John XXIII, MATER ET MAGISTRA.

Start Today!

Today the world is wide open. Its needs and its problems press upon us from all sides. People in Vietnam, in Harlem, in India are our neighbors. Radio, TV, newspapers force us to SEE. But nationalism, prejudice, snobbishness can keep us from being AWARE. Our first duty as Christian students is to become AWARE so that we may learn to CARE.

44. *Did you view the newscast yesterday or read the paper? Which particular areas of the world are causing concern?*

45. *Select one of the following areas for group study. Contact at least one organization which is actively engaged in servicing needs and report on their effectiveness:*

   a. Peace b. Poverty c. Ecumenism d. Treatment of minority groups

46. *If God can establish His kingdom without the help of man, why does He want us to be involved in the task of redeeming the world?*

47. *Jack says, "The world is changing so fast that no one knows what it will be like in twenty years. We may even be wiped out by a thermonuclear attack. So why should we prepare for a future which even the scientists cannot predict?" Ann replies, "The world will change, but people will still be pretty much the same. Their values, purposes in life, and the important things will remain the same." Discuss their points of view.*

48. *What, if anything, do your activities as a student, your co-curricular interests, and your part-time job contribute to the work of creation? Do sloppy study habits, cheating, and poor workmanship dissipate the energies of creation?*

Changing Backdrop for the Eucharist

Because the saving acts of God are so rich in meaning, the Church makes them into a revolving background for the celebration of the Eucharist. The heart of the Eucharist is always our union with Christ in His death and resurrection, but through the seasons of the Church Year the Mystery of Christ comes to us in a succession of colors, like the pure ray of light viewed in its spectrum. Thus the Christian, who though saved is always being saved, meets Christ under various guises and receives His life again and again in myriad ways.

The Church Year is divided into two unequal parts—the Christmas cycle and the Easter cycle. Each of these in turn has a time of preparation, a time of celebration, and a time of thanksgiving and reflection centering around the mystery of the Incarnation and the Redemption. This is the seasonal or temporal cycle. Outside it is the sanctoral cycle, commemorating the feasts of Our Lady and the Saints.

49. *Draw a circle representing the Church Year and its different seasons. Use the liturgical colors (purple, white or gold, and green) to show the divisions of the seasons. Draw another circle outside the first and mark on it your favorite feasts of Our Lady and the saints.*

162

It's Your Move!

1. How did the sacred writer know about God's relations with man in pre-history?

2. What is the central message of Genesis 1 to 11?

3. Since the Genesis account of creation resembles the pagan legends, how can it be an inspired book?

4. Describe the universe as the biblical writers knew it.

5. What religious truth is contained in the first chapter of Genesis?

6. In what sense is man made to the image and likeness of God?

7. What limitation was placed upon man's activity at creation?

8. What place does sex have in the plan of God?

9. If God is good and everything He made is good, how do you account for the evil that is in the world?

10. Distinguish between temptation and sin.

11. What are the effects of sin on man and his world?

12. What evidence do we have of our need of redemption?

13. What religious truth is conveyed in the story of Cain and Abel? of Noah and the Flood? of the Tower of Babel?

14. What ideas are common to the Prologue of Genesis and the Prologue of St. John's Gospel?

15. Why can Christ be called the New Adam?

16. What is the New Creation brought about in Christ?

17. Show how the principle: Matter + Spirit = New Creation can be applied to human affairs; to the Christian; to Christ.

18. How can each Christian help to redeem the world?

19. What can a ninth grader do to prepare himself to participate in the redemption of the world?

20. Why does the Church observe the various seasons of the Church Year?

Reflection

THE CHRISTIAN AND THE WORLD

Every age,
every state of life,
every vocation
has the obligation to proclaim
in its own situation, work, and actions
the consecration of the world
that has already begun in
Christ's incarnation
so that the world may be
transfigured,
that is, healed and perfected
in Christ's glory.
Every Christian,
that is, everyone who applies to himself
this title taken from Christ's divine office,
binds himself thereby
to help bring
Christ's work
to perfection,
namely, to gloriously renew
himself,
humanity,
and the world.
                    --Walter Durig, THE CHRISTIAN AND THE WORLD

And the Word
was made flesh,
and dwelt among
us.

And we saw his glory
--glory as of the only-begotten of the Father--
full of grace
and of truth.
                    --John 1:14

Chapter 13 -
God's Universal Concern

A Freshman Once Said
Is God a Catholic?

"You know what I mean--are Catholics an in-group? Does God love them more than He loves others? Are all the front seats in heaven reserved for Catholics? What about my friend who is a Protestant? She doesn't go to church every Sunday, but she's a good kid. And what about Abe Cohen down the street? He doesn't even believe in Christ, but he's more faithful to his religion than I am to mine. Should we try to make them all Catholics, or doesn't it really matter to what religion you belong?"

1. Discuss: Parents should love all their children equally, but it is not necessary to treat them all exactly alike.

2. Our Declaration of Independence says that all men are equal. In what sense is this true and in what sense is it not true?

3. Discuss: God will judge all men according to the same standard.

Light from the Old Testament

When the Jews returned from the exile in Babylon, they were very determined that the covenant would not be broken again. In fact, they erected such a strong barrier between themselves and their Gentile neighbors that they were inclined to forget that the very reason God had chosen them in the first place was that they might be a "light to the Gentiles." Some became snobbish and intolerant, looking with scorn on the peoples who were not as favored by God as they had been. They concluded that those who were excluded from the Chosen People were also excluded from God's love and favor. During this time two stories were written to re-emphasize the fact of God's love for all men and of Israel's mission to the nations.

165

Do not press me

to leave you

to turn back

from following you;

for wherever you go,

I will go ...

The Good Pagan

Book of Ruth

Ruth is a lovely Gentile girl from Moab, who became the great grandmother of King David and thereby an ancestor of the Messiah. Her story is taken from the period of the conquest of Chanaan, and Ruth emerges as a true heroine who "lived happily ever after."

4. Why do you think Ruth chose to stay with her mother-in-law?

5. Note Booz's greeting to the harvesters. What will you answer the next time it is addressed to you?

6. Booz was a good man who kept the Law. Find evidence for this in Leviticus 19:9-10 and Deuteronomy 24:19.

7. Read Deuteronomy 25:5-10 for an explanation of the levirate law.

8. What words of Noemi's are applied to Our Lady in the Mass for the Feast of the Seven Sorrows?

9. Ruth is a favorite subject of artists. There are pictures of her by Murillo, Poussin and Van Dyck. What did Keats say of her in his poem, "Ode to a Nightingale"?

10. Dramatize the scene that you think best brings out the beautiful qualities of Ruth's character.

The Unmerciful Prophet

Jonah is the name of a prophet who lived in the days of Jeroboam II (750 B.c.),but this story about him was not written until 400 years later. It is a biting satire on those Jews who thought that God was their exclusive property. The unknown author presents a striking contrast between the narrow, self-righteous prophet and the humble, penitent pagans.

11. Why didn't Jonah want to preach to Nineve? Cf. 4:1-3.

12. Who is the hero of the story? Compare his action with that of the Father in the Prodigal Son. Cf. Luke 15:25-32.

13. The author presents the pagans in a very favorable light. What evidence do you find in the story of their good dispositions?

14. The story is honored by being made a sign of Our Lord's resurrection. Cf. Matthew 12:38-41.

"There comes with the reading of Jonah, a great sense of the divine joke God has played... The little figure of Jonah... standing jubilantly with arms extended in 'Alleluia!' beside his joyful f i s h...seems to shout, 'You men, little and insignificant, rejoice! He has paid a great price for you. He has taken your nothingness and bought it with His own worth and you have become priceless. He has turned all His pain and yours into blessings. He has made tragedy into comedy and joy has come out of sorrow, life has come out of death. Rejoice, little children, for God loves you!' It is a lovely joke--God loving man so much."
--Mary Reed Newland, THE FAMILY AND THE BIBLE.

Though Dark the Night

The tiny province of Juda had a series of masters as the domination of the world passed from one conqueror to another--Nabuchodonosor of Babylonia, Cyrus of Persia, Alexander of Greece and his successors. The Jews paid their taxes to whoever happened to be the top man, while the Sanhedrin continued to control the local government. But when Antiochus IV came to the Syrian throne in 174 B.C., he wasn't satisfied with collecting taxes from the Jews--he wanted them brain-washed of Judaism and converted to Hellenism.

The violent attack on God's People forced them to make a decision. They had to be for, or against, the things their faith taught them--no one could be lukewarm. There were many apostates--and many martyrs. Mattathias and his five sons, the Machabees, led the revolt which for a short time brought the Jews independence from Syria.

15. Prepare a report for the class on Hellenism. Use 2 Machabees 4:7-17 for an example of the "fifth column."

16. How successful was Alexander in his campaign to spread Greek culture? What evidence of Greek culture do you find in our civilization? What evidence of Jewish culture do you find? Is it a good balance?

17. Discuss the incident of the people who would not defend themselves on the Sabbath? Do you agree with Mattathias' decision?

18. The Assideans or Hasidim, "the pious ones," (2:42-44) were the devout Jews who refused to compromise with Hellenism. They later became known as Pharisees. Prepare a class report on what they came to stand for. Cf. Catholic Biblical Encyclopedia (New Testament).

...How Bright Your Light!

Men, women and children--all were represented in the heroic people who gave their lives rather than break their covenant with the God who had always been true to His people.

19. There are special stores today where devout Jews buy "kosher" food. Look up "dietary laws" in the Catholic Biblical Encyclopedia (New Testament), and tell the class what these laws include.

20. The description of the mother of the seven Machabees (2 Machabees 7:21) is a classic one. Write a paragraph explaining what it means.

21. What do we ask for in the Prayer of the Mass for the feast of the Machabees? What people today in the same situation as the Machabees especially need that prayer?

22. Robert Kennedy, in an address to the American Jewish Congress, said that the American armed forces all over the world were there "for the same reason that the Machabees stood their ground against Antiochus--for human dignity and freedom." What did he mean by the comparison?

Light from the New Testament

A Great Privilege...

The Jews' resistance to Hellenism drew them together as God's Chosen People. But from the emphasis placed on their favored position, there gradually developed not only a strict segregation from their Gentile neighbors, but also an attitude of superiority toward them. The gospels give evidence that this situation still prevailed in the time of Our Lord.

23. In what way is our problem of racial segregation similar to this situation?

Matthew 15:21-28 - Jesus' apparent harshness to this pagan woman became the occasion by which she gave public evidence of the depth of her faith and the strength of her love for her afflicted daughter. She thereby earned a great compliment from Jesus and the admiration of all those who read the Gospel.

24. Jesus confirmed the Jews' belief that they were special to God. St. Paul (Romans 11:25-29) says that God will always love them and that eventually they, too, will be part of His Kingdom.

Matthew 8:5-13 - Jesus readily offered to go to the house of the Roman centurion. When the man protested, Jesus marvelled at his goodness and said that many pagans were more pleasing to God than some of the Chosen People.

25. What custom was Jesus willing to ignore for the sake of the centurion?

26. What admirable traits of character can you detect in the centurion?

Luke 14:15-24 - Because the invited guests were "too busy" to come to the great supper, the poor and the outcasts were given an opportunity to enjoy the feasts.

27. Compare Luke's story of the feast with Matthew's (22:1-10). What point is each trying to make?

...And a Grave Responsibility!

The realization that the fulfillment of the Lord's desire for the salvation of ALL men was, to some extent, in the hands of His followers dawned on the Church gradually. Eventually they realized that the call to be a Christian was at the same time a call to be a missionary.

John 10:14-16 and 17:14-26 - Jesus sends His followers into the world that by their witness of His love they may bring His other sheep to know and love the Father as He does.

28. Give some evidence that Christ's followers are not one. What is the main cause of disunity?

29. Discuss the relative merits of a person or an idea as a bond of unity. Is your Student Council better united by its Constitution or by a dynamic president?

Acts 10 - This passage describes the Pentecost of the Gentiles. The little group of Jews intent on bringing the knowledge of Christ to their own people now became truly catholic with a message of salvation directed to ALL MEN.

30. Notice that Peter is instructed to ignore the very thing for which the seven Machabees gave their lives, the Jewish dietary laws. How can a practice that is very wrong at one time be permissible at another?

31. Which sentence from Peter's speech should guide our attitude toward people of other religions?

Truths We Share

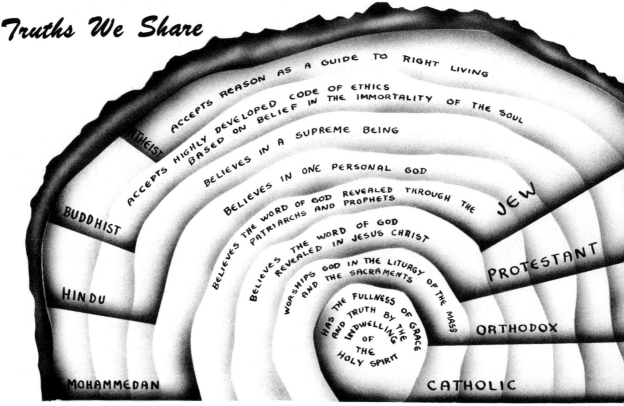

<u>2 John 1:7-11</u> - This is the other side of the coin. While Peter is instructed in the respect that is due to people of other faiths, John counsels the Christians to cherish the "doctrine of Christ" which they had received and under no circumstances to allow it to be mixed with error.

32. *How is it possible to observe both these instructions? Can we have a great respect for the faith of others and still want to share our faith with them?*

So You See...

We do honestly believe that Christ has given to His Church the fullness of His truth, but that does not mean that other faiths do not share that truth in varying degrees. Neither does it mean that every Catholic is automatically a better person than a non-Catholic. Because we live in a pluralistic (composed of followers of different religions) society, it is important that we learn to associate with people of other faiths avoiding both INTOLERANCE and INDIFFERENTISM.

We Have Been Given the Truth... Romans 2:12-16

Although as Catholics we have access to the fullness of grace and truth, we are not thereby superior to those of other faiths. They also share much of this truth and sometimes they make better use of it than we do. God will judge us finally not on how much we know, but on how well we have lived in accord with what we know.

33. *Study the diagram to discover how many truths we share with other religions.*

A genuine respect for the ideas and ideals of other faiths is the first step toward achieving the unity for which Christ prayed. The Second Vatican Council issued four important documents to guide our efforts to clear away the barriers that separate us from others who are also God's children. They are:

   a. The Declaration on Religious Liberty
   b. The Declaration on non-Christian Religions

c.   The Decree on Ecumenism
d.   The Constitution on the Church

34. *From OUTLINES OF THE 16 DOCUMENTS, VATICAN II by Virginia Mary Heffernan, (The America Press) prepare a report for the class on the main idea contained in each of the statements.*

35. *Discuss the wisdom of these activities in promoting unity:*

  a. *Try to learn about what others believe.*
  b. *Be prepared to defend your own faith in an argument.*
  c. *Join with those of other faiths in projects to improve your neighborhood.*
  d. *Be ready to admit that the Church has made mistakes.*
  e. *Listen with sympathy to what others think and believe.*
  f. *Be willing to compromise on what the Church teaches.*

36. *Discuss: Our motto in ecumenical affairs ought to be "Unity but not uniformity."*

"Whoever they are (the laity), they are called upon as living members of Christ to expend all their energy for the growth of the Church and its continuous sanctification, since this very energy is a gift of the Creator and a blessing of the Redeemer." --THE CONSTITUTION ON THE CHURCH.

...Not for Ourselves, but for Others !   Matthew 5:13-16
                                                      28:19-20

        With the gift of faith comes the obligation to "proclaim the Lord Jesus until He comes." We must share our faith with others not through arguments or "religious imperialism," but by the clear evidence in our words and deeds of what knowing Christ has done for us. When Catholics exhibit joy in living, strength in suffering, and active concern for their fellowmen, their witness to Christ and the Church is irresistible. When we add to this a real enthusiasm for the faith, we are the missionaries that Christ intended each of His followers to be.

37. Why do you think so many young Americans are interested in the work of the Peace Corps? Are there similar opportunities to share your faith in Christ? Do you think American Catholic youth have a greater enthusiasm for the American way of living than they have for the Christian way of life?

38. Father Eugene Zimmer, S.J., some five years ago, founded at the University of San Francisco a Lay Theologian program to prepare laymen for work in parishes. What are some of the things these men could do to "proclaim the Lord Jesus"?

39. Jonah's sojourn in the depths of the sea, Jesus' silence in the tomb, and our plunge into the waters of baptism--all are a prelude to a new and better life. Did you come from the baptismal font a "Jonah-Christian" or a "Pauline Christian"? What is the difference between the two? Cf. 1 Tim. 2:4.

40. If we are reluctant like Jonah "to preach to Nineve," are our reasons the same as Jonah's?

41. Divide the class into groups; allow six to eight minutes discussion, then have one member of each group report on the following:

   a. Besides the priestly and religious vocation is there a lay vocation, one that requires witnessing for Christ in the world? Discuss specific examples.
   b. How do we fulfill our "witness vocation" as students? How can we be apostles here and now?

Projecting the faith and not merely protecting it - The Church must never again pretend to be the loaf, the meat, the only light--rather it must be the leaven that lifts, the salt that savors and preserves, the light that shines brighter than all the rest.

Seeking the truth rather than claiming it--As Christians we believe that the Truth became Incarnate in humanity. Now we must strive to incarnate ever more perfectly and ever more relevantly Christ in our society. This is never an accomplished fact but an ever continuing process. The truth of the Church lies in Christ. But we shall never possess the fullness of truth--the fullness of Christ--till the Last Day.
                    --Priests of San Miguelito, APOSTOLATE

"The Mass Is Ended! Go..."

The Mass is our constantly renewed pledge of loyalty to Christ. Ordinarily we express love by words, gifts and actions. The Liturgy of the Word is our dialogue of love with God; the Liturgy of the Sacrifice is our exchange of gifts. Then as the ceremony draws to a close, the celebrant turns to us and says in effect: "Go now, and prove that the friendship which you pledged in word and symbolized in gift is no empty sign. Let all your words and deeds proclaim that what you said and did here in this assembly was real. Go *...and live the Mass!*

39. *The Mass might be compared to the football team that meets with the coach in the locker-room during the half-time. How many similarities can you find?*

The constant action of the Mass is expressed by the prayers of the Ordinary; the Propers of the Mass reflect the changing mood of the various feasts and the liturgical year. The prayers of the Propers are of three kinds:

    a. Meditation Chants - I n t r o i t, Gradual, Offertory, Communion
       Made up of psalm verses or brief selections from Scripture
    b. Prayer of the Assembly, Prayer over the Gifts, and Prayer after Communion
       Petitions composed by the Church, offered to God in name of all the people through Christ
    c. Readings - Epistle or Lesson from the Old Testament and the gospel

40. *Compose the Propers for a Mass to Obtain an Apostolic Spirit. Study the forms of the various parts from a Mass in your missal and model your prayers on them. Choose appropriate Scripture passages for the chants and readings. You may find it helpful to consult the Encyclopedic Dictionary of the Bible, the Biblical Index, or the Index in the back of your Bible under such topics as apostle, faith, witness, etc..*

It's Your Move!

1. What bad effect resulted from the Jews' determination to protect their people from contact with pagans?

2. What theme is emphasized in the Book of Ruth and the Book of Jonah?

3. What is the literary form of the Book of Jonah? What is the religious teaching it conveys?

4. Why were the Jews so opposed to Hellenism?

5. What is the role of persecution in God's plan?

6. What was the general attitude of the Jews toward the Gentiles at the time of Our Lord? What was His attitude toward the pagans?

7. What is the significance of the vision Peter had of the unclean animals?

8. What principles should guide our relations with those of other faiths?

9. What truths do we hold in common with Protestants? with Jews?

10. What should be our attitude toward the faith we have been given?

11. How can we live the Mass?

12. Give the purpose of the Propers of the Mass and describe the various prayers they contain.

Reflection

In one of his plays, Jean Anouilh describes the last judgment as he sees it. The good are densely clustered at the gate of heaven, eager to march in, sure of their reserved seats, keyed up and bursting with impatience.

All at once, a rumor starts spreading: "It seems He's going to forgive those others, too!" For a minute, everyone's dumbfounded. They look at one another in disbelief, gasping and sputtering. "After all the trouble I went through!" "If only I'd known..." "I just can't get over it!"Exasperated, they work themselves into a fury and start cursing God; and at that very instant they're damned. That was the final judgment, you see.

They judged themselves, excommunicated themselves. Love appeared, and they refused to acknowledge it. "We don't know this man." "We don't approve of a heaven that's open to every Tom, Dick, and Harry." "We can't love a God who loves so foolishly." And because they didn't love LOVE, they didn't recognize Him. Do we love LOVE? Do we like the way He loves? Do we believe that He alone knows how to love, that He alone can teach us to love? --L. Evely, THAT MAN IS YOU.

Further Insights

The Book of Daniel

An unknown scribe wove together stories about a national hero, Daniel, and put into his mouth "prophecies" which dealt not with the future, but with his own day. He used the background of the Babylonian Exile both to avert the suspicions of the Syrians and to encourage his suffering fellow-citizens to be faithful to God's law. In the light of Babylonia he showed the people the meaning of the persecution inflicted on them. What God had done for Daniel, He would do for them!

The first part of the book consists of a series of "midrash," that is, free treatments of historical themes and personalities, the purpose of which is to edify, not to record accurately.

Song of the Flames

3:1-97

The author presents a grand spectacle of the triumphant power of God which even Nabuchodonosor had to recognize.

41. The Benedicite (Cf. vv. 52-90) is the official thanksgiving after Holy Mass. It is also recited in Lauds of the Divine Office. Choose some phrases that appeal to you to say as you walk to or from school--or make up some that fit the occasion.

42. For the first time in Old Testament writing we have clear references to the angels as we know them (Cf. vv. 49, 92, 95). Collect the information about angels from these passages in the Book of Daniel: 6:23, 3:55, 7:9, 8:16, 9:21, 10:13.

The Lions' Den

Chapter 6

This story is a treasured part of world literature and a beautiful testimony to our need for frequent prayer.

43. Has your fidelity to the service of God ever caused you to be "thrown to the lions"? When it happens again, remember Daniel 6:27-28.

44. The girls in Polly's crowd decided they would "get even" with Donna who, they thought, was the cause of their getting an extra English assignment. They agreed to have a "Hate-Donna-Week" during which they would make her as miserable as possible by little snubs and slights. Kathy felt uncomfortable about it, but decided that since "everyone was doing it", she would too. Does Daniel have a message for her?

The Chaste Susanna
Chapter 13

This is a simple and charming story which illustrates Daniel's wisdom as a judge. The wicked elders could be either the lustful Hellenizers or the Jews who were in sympathy with them.

45. Does Susanna remind you of a recently canonized saint? Compare Susanna's words (vv. 22-23) with hers.

Chapter 14 - God's Promise Fulfilled

A Freshman Once Said
When will I be my best self?

"I used to think that when I was sixteen my life would have reached its climax, and that when I got to be twenty-one I might just as well 'throw in the sponge.' But the older I get, the farther off I put the age when people seem 'to have arrived.' Now I'm beginning to wonder whether I ever will. Deep down within me I see so many possibilities, but at the rate I'm going I don't think a lifetime is going to be long enough to bring them to the surface and to put them in working order. Will the 'becoming' ever turn into 'being'?"

1. How does the progress your family makes affect your own development?

2. How does your individual progress affect the advancement of your family?

3. Give some evidence that society is going through a "becoming" process.

4. Did Christ redeem the world or just the people?

5. Is Redemption an accomplished fact or a gradual process?

Light from the Old Testament

Land of the Dead

For centuries the Israelites retained the depressing views of the after-life that Abraham had learned in his native Babylonia where those who died were thought to have descended into the nether world. The Abode of the Dead ("Sheol") was characterized by darkness, dust and silence. Situated in the depths of the earth, it was the last resting place of all men with no distinction between the good and the evil.

6. Compare the Hebrew "Sheol" (Cf. Encyclopedia Dictionary of the Bible, "Dead, Abode of") with the Greek "Hades."

A Door to Eternal Life

2 Machabees 12:38-46
7:30-40

In the last two centuries before Christ, hope in God's fidelity to the Covenant blossomed into certainty that He would continue to love His people even after death. They were also led to the realization that in Sheol there are sections for the just and for the wicked.

7. Consult the following texts to discover the various names by which the after-life came to be known: Luke 16:22, Luke 23:43, Matthew 12:40, and 1 Peter 3:19.

The Judgment of the Nations

Joel 2:27-3:5
4:11-21

The victory of God and His people over their enemies was long delayed. But the prophets assured the people that the Day of the Lord would surely come and that through His power they would achieve their destiny as a nation.

8. When was this prophecy fulfilled? Cf. Acts 2:14-24.

The Heavenly Kingdom

Daniel 7

Gradually the expected Kingdom came to be regarded as something which would come down to earth from heaven at the end of time to be the dwelling-place of the just. Writings that describe this event are called apocalyptic. This is a style of writing suited to a time of crisis to faith brought about by oppression or persecution. By the vivid presentation of the display of power and glory attendant on the Lord's victory over His enemies, the author strives to inspire confidence in the eventual fulfillment of God's promises. Looking to the distant future, he confidently shows God's final intervention in history and its glorious outcome.

Because the material is usually presented in the form of visions, the sacred writer uses mystic numbers, mysterious symbols, and strange images. Unless the reader has a key to the symbolism used, it is practically impossible to get the message. The apocalyptic passage from Daniel has had a very real influence on Christianity.

9. Using the code given below, interpret Daniel 7:

   lion - Babylonian Empire   bear - Empire of the Medes

   winged leopard - Persian Empire which had four great conquerors in a row

   beast with the iron teeth - Macedonian Empire of Alexander the Great

   ten horns - Seleucid kings   little horns - Antiochus IV

   Ancient One - God   son of man - God's people

10. Write an Apocalypse for the Christian martyrs who suffered under the Roman emperors. Remember that it involves a vision of God's final victory expressed in symbolic language. Be sure to give the key to your symbolism.

180

Light from the New Testament

The Kingdom -- Present and Future

The Gospel announces that the Kingdom, God's Rule over the world and men, has begun. The Day of the Lord has dawned in the coming of Jesus. This is His final intervention in history. The seed He has planted will grow and expand, and He will return to harvest His crop.

Matthew 3:1-17 - God's Reign on earth begins in this one man who relates perfectly to His Father and to His fellowmen. He is beloved of God and filled with the Spirit.

11. *Explain what is meant by Jesus' words, "The kingdom of God is within you." (Luke 17:21)*

Acts 2:29-36 - When Jesus is exalted at the Right Hand of God and sends His Spirit on His followers, God's Reign on earth is extended to them. This is the beginning of the end of sin's dominion over God's creatures. The Kingdom grows with every person who accepts Jesus as Lord and thereby shares in His power of loving.

12. *When do we receive the Spirit? Why does God use things and other men to give us the Spirit?*

Luke 21:5-28 - The fullness of the Kingdom is still in the future. When the struggle with evil has been successfully completed, Christ will return. This glorious coming of Christ, the "Parousia", is compared to the magnificent procession of the oriental king visiting one of his towns or provinces. The sacred writers resort to apocalyptic writing to encourage the early Christian community suffering from the hostility of the Jewish leaders. They see in the anticipated fulfillment of Christ's prophecy about the destruction of Jerusalem a type of His eventual victory over all who oppose Him.

13. *What evidence of the apocalyptic style can you find in the passage?*

14. *The early Christians took the idea of Christ's Second Coming so seriously that some of them thought it was useless to settle down to making a living. Read St. Paul's rebuke to them in 2 Thessalonians 2:1-12 and 3:6-12.*

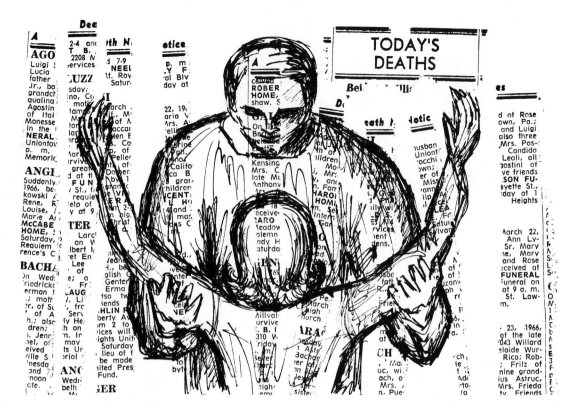

Our Personal Parousia

Most of us will have our own personal meeting with the Son of Man before His Final Coming, and in each of these bits of human history the pattern of God's kingdom is worked out. The New Testament is more concerned with the overall view of the "last things," but whatever is said of the general resurrection and judgment can be applied to the individual events that lead to it.

Luke 12:35-48 - Death is the enemy of God and of man, which entered the world with sin. In spite of our frequent contacts with it, death remains a mystery because no one can speak of it from first-hand experience. Scripture tells us only that we are as certain of meeting death as we are uncertain of when and where the meeting will take place.

15. *Write a theme on how you would spend your last twenty-four hours if you were told you had just one more day to live.*

1 Corinthians 15:20-28 and 54-57 - On Calvary Jesus met and conquered our two great foes--death and sin. He entered the enemy territory and took it captive. For His followers, the dead-end street of death has become the gateway to eternal life.

16. *Make a symbolic drawing of Christ's words in Apocalypse 1:17-18.*

"It was by dying that He changed the very essence of death. Death was an ending, it is now a beginning; it was the destruction of life, it is now its very condition; it was separation from God, it is now the way to union with Him. For a Christian to live he must first die; for him to share in the Resurrection he must first partake of the Death of Christ."
    --Stanley B. Marrow, S.J., DEATH FOR A CHRISTIAN.

Matthew 25:31-46 - It seems that in the long run our eternal destiny is going to depend on how we answer just one question: "How did y o u treat other people?"

17. To offset the bad publicity that teenagers get, make a collection of pictures or newspaper and magazine articles about young people practicing t h e corporal works of mercy.

1 Corinthians 13:8-13 - Although the Scripture often speaks of what we must do to get to heaven, it doesn't really tell us much of what heaven is like, except to assure us that both we ourselves and the material world will be renewed in the depths of our being. St. Augustine (CITY OF GOD, 22.30) tells us that "we shall have rest and shall see, we shall see and shall love, we shall love and shall praise." In other words, we shall be engaged in very familiar and very satisfying activity.

18. Discuss what idea of heaven the sacred writer is conveying in the following images:

        a. Apocalypse 7:17   c. Matthew 22:2
        b. Matthew 13:44   d. Apocalypse 21:2-4

So You See . . .

Your desire to "become" what you are blends in perfectly with the great forward thrust of your Christian faith. The world God made was good, but far from realizing all its potential. God willed that the process of creation should continue under man's direction and to a great extent be dependent on his energy and initiative. So the aching for fulfillment that you feel is shared by every creature.

19. Review God's commission to men in Genesis 1:28-29.

20. What are some of the outstanding things men have accomplished in this regard in the past ten years? What are some of the challenges that men still face in their task of "subduing" the earth?

The Spirit of Renewal

Romans 8:18-27

Sin upset the orderly relation that existed between men and nature and made man's work of bringing the world and himself to completion difficult and frustrating. But when Jesus rose from the dead and was filled with the glory of God, a New Creation took place. From that moment victory over the destructive forces let loose in the world by sin was assured. It is only a matter of time until our Brother Christ will have communicated to us, and through us to the world, the fullness of life and love which He enjoys. Christ began His work of transforming us into a New Creation at baptism. At the Parousia even our bodies will be totally penetrated and renewed by His life-giving Spirit.

21. What can we do to assist the Spirit of Christ in His work of renewing us?

A Here-and-Now Redemption

Are you a "hereafter" Christian? Are you one who thinks that he has to take time out occasionally from the real business of living to fulfill his "spiritual" duties so that he can attain salvation in the "next world"? If so, you have missed the point completely. Your redemption (or lack of it) is a continuing process that is involved in everything you do or say. It can be stated very briefly in two simple questions.

a. What kind of a person are you becoming?
b. What kind of a world are you making?

22. Discuss the relationship between these two aspects of your role in redemption. Are they equally important? Have we in the past overemphasized one or the other?

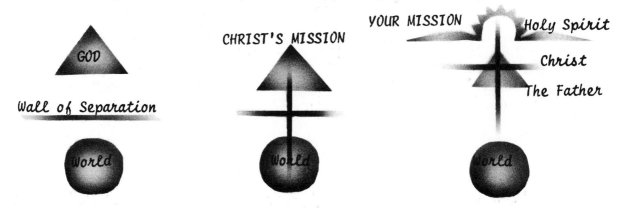

184

23. *Using the diagram show how we share in Christ's work of redeeming the world.*

> The wonders of the Last Day are not to be understood as a cataclysmic marvel wrought by God alone. The glory of that 'day' is rather the completion of a saving work in which man plays a dynamic role.
>
> --B. Ahern, NEW HORIZONS

Building a Better World

At the end of time Christ will present a Perfect World to His Father, a world that men have helped Him build. What contribution will you make to this tremendous task? Whether you are a mechanic or a nuclear scientist, a fileclerk or a social worker, you can bring the world and society a little nearer to the perfection for which it is destined. When you perform this work with love and dedication, you help to purge away its impurities and hasten its fulfillment in Christ.

Your specific role in the earth's redemption may be in one of two directions: horizontal or vertical. You may dedicate yourself to the WORLD AS IT IS and work to maintain it; this will require faithful service and large hearted compassion for the needs of others. Or you may prefer to serve the WORLD AS IT WILL BE; this will require depths of thinking and heights of imagination, vision and initiative.

24. *Discuss these pairs of occupations with regard to their direction to the world, their similarity and difference:*

    a. mother   b. doctor   c. tool maker   d. nurse
       housekeeper   scientist   tool designer   teacher

    e. hairdresser   f. lawyer   g. architect
       beautician   senator   construction engineer

25. *Discuss the various attitudes toward their work displayed by these three laborers on a construction job. When asked what they were doing, Pete said, "Making a living, and a lousy one at that!" James said, "Building a house. That's pretty obvious!" John said, "Making a home for a young couple and their children!"*

26. *You are not too young to do a little thinking about how you will help to "redeem" the world. Try to find yourself in the WHO I AM column; then select some profession in the related column in which you could realize your abilities.*

WHO I AM

I am interested in the "WHY" of the world about me; curious about new things; interested in the discovery and realization of truth; intrigued by people and situations.

I have a sense of others' needs; I am sympathetic and concerned about any type of suffering; I desire to help Christ in His needy members.

I am creative and like to explore new ideas, develop new ideas from old ones; evolve new inventions; work at developing solutions to social or political problems; create beauty or make things "be."

I am interested in promoting justice; in searching for truth and working for right.

I am interested in people and in their development. I have a belief in people and a desire to help them to become their best selves.

I am interested in entertaining others; in creating pleasure and happiness for them.

I am interested in exploring new frontiers where men have not gone before; the unknown worlds of space, of machines, of science interest me.

In a short paragraph describe some specific field in which you could contribute to our world.

WHERE I COULD BECOME MYSELF AND HELP CREATE A BETTER WORLD

Fields of science, medicine, mathematics, philosophy, psychology, history, economics

Vocation of government service, labor relations, journalism, social work, medicine, sociology

Vocation to art, architecture, journalism, engineering, political science, television, literature

Vocation to law, government, community agencies

Vocation to teaching, counseling, coaching, leader of youth groups

Vocation to acting, lecturing, singing, writing

Vocation to technological fields, space exploration

27. From the hands that plant the wheat to those that raise the consecrated Host, many hands join in the awesome task of bringing Christ to earth. Express this inspiring truth graphically--by pictures, drawing, poetry, etc.

Our Final "Yes"

2 Corinthians 5:1-10

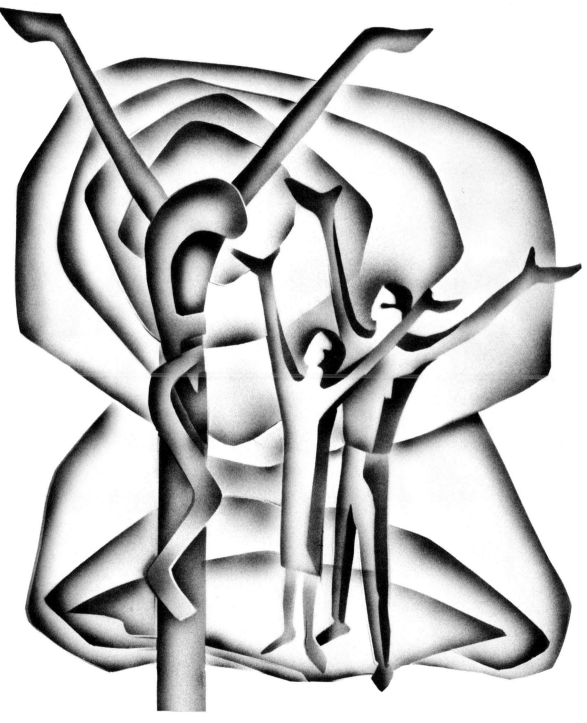

The life of a Christian is a "growing-up" in Christ. Each choice that he makes helps to set the pattern of what he is becoming. Each year that he lives shows a deeper concern for his fellowmen and a stronger attachment to the things of God. And when the moment of death arrives, he makes the final choice, as he has made all the others. All his life he has been dying in small ways to the selfish demands that oppose God's ways; the pattern has been set and death is merely his final "yes" to God. He says with Christ, "Father, into Thy hands I commend my spirit," and with Him enters into the vision of God and a new and perfect life where he is truly himself.

If during his life he has wavered between selfishness and generosity, it will be a painful process to make this once-for-all commitment to God. He will suffer in this purging of selfishness; he will be in purgatory.

If, God forbid, the pattern that gradually emerged in his day-by-day choices is a commitment to his own interests, he will ratify that choice, and in so doing he will face an eternity of his own company--without God or his fellowmen--and the bitter loneliness of those who never learned to love.

28. *Discuss the various images by which the suffering of hell is described in the Bible: Matthew 25:41; Mark 9:46-47; Matthew 25:30; 2 Thessalonians 1:9*

A New Day

Apocalypse 21:1-8

A true Christian looks forward to the coming of the Lord Jesus with joy. The LAST DAY will be one of judgment when the veil will be removed and all men will see the total meaning of the history of salvation. But it will also be the FIRST DAY of an era of truth and love, of justice and mercy, of peace, of fulfillment. On this Day, the heavens will open, Christ will stand in the radiant splendor of His beauty. He will invite all of heaven to enter the world, to transform it into the Palace of God. Heaven will be on earth and earth will be in heaven. His Kingdom will have come!

29. *When you say the Apostles' Creed what do you mean by the phrase, "I believe in the resurrection of the body"?*

The kingdom will be a world that is RECONCILED, for the perfect order IN GOD will pour out a perfect order among things, a harmony that will spread to the tiniest realities.
--Yves Congar, LAY PEOPLE IN THE CHURCH

The Heavenly Banquet

Both the Old and the New Testament writers speak of the Kingdom of God as a banquet, a meal where at the expense of the host the guests feast on the finest delicacies of his house and enjoy the spirit of fellowship that characterizes such an assembly. The Eucharist prepares us for the great unending meal in Our Father's house, for in the Risen Christ whom we receive, the source of eternal life and glory is present to us. When we gather around the Table of the Lord united by our faith in Christ, the reality of the Kingdom is already present, though hidden, wrapped in the mysterious action of the liturgy.

30. Reflect for a few moments on the profound realities made present in the Eucharist and then say together: "O sacred Banquet in which Christ is received, the memory of His passion renewed, the soul filled with grace, and a pledge of future glory is given to us."

31. The Christian attitude toward death is most beautifully expressed in the ancient prayers of the Mass for the Dead. In your Missal read the Preface and the prayer that is sung as the funeral procession leaves the church, and show how faith in Christ takes the "sting" out of death.

It's Your Move!   Checkmate!

1. Describe the earliest Israelite concept of the afterlife.

2. What new developments took place in this regard toward the end of Old Testament times?

3. What did the prophets mean by the Day of the Lord?

4. What are the characteristics of apocalyptic writing?

5. What is the New Testament concept of the Day of the Lord?

6. In what sense is the Kingdom of God present? In what sense is it still in the future?

7. What does the New Testament tell us about death?

8. What does the New Testament tell us about heaven?

9. How is the Resurrection of Christ the beginning of a New Creation?

10. Why isn't it enough for a Christian to be concerned about "saving his soul"?

11. How should a Christian regard his work?

12. What is meant by the saying, "As we live, so shall we die"?

13. Why should we look forward without fear and even with joy to the Last Day?

14. How is the Eucharist a "pledge of future glory"?

189

Reflection

And so you are on your way to high adventure, making a new world. By your baptism and your confirmation you have been called to be the leaven by which Christ's redemptive power becomes operative in the world. In your daily call to Christian living you are called--

LIKE ABRAHAM, TO LEAVE...

to leave the pleasant security of the known for the unknown adventure of faith.

LIKE JACOB, TO LOVE...

to love your family and friends in such a way that in your generous love for them you find Christ.

LIKE MOSES, TO LEAD...

to lead others to Christ by stimulating their interest in knowing why God comes first in your life.

LIKE DAVID, TO RULE...

to rule over your 1,001 desires and urges and little rebellions, and so steer a straight course to God.

LIKE JEREMIAH, TO SUFFER...

to suffer the price of bearing witness to Christ in your everyday world of friends, ballgames, textbooks, dates, and cars.

You can live your life to the fullest by bringing

to the world of men

to your world in school,

at work,

in the gym,

in the home,

values which are so animated with Christ that

YOU STAND AS CHRIST...YOU ARE HIS WITNESS...HIS HANDS...HIS VOICE...HIS HEART.

MY LORD IS LONG A COMIN'

Sister Germaine, Glenmary Sister

REFRAIN:
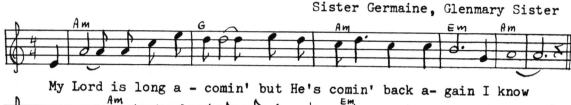

My Lord is long a - comin' but He's comin' back a- gain I know

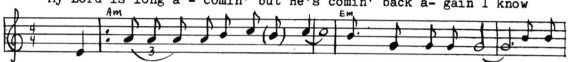

1. When - ever I see a woolly lamb   jump - in' in a field   It re-
        Wouldn't he leave all   search for the one   And if he
                ninety-nine And/   who was lost,

minds me of Him.
found him, wouldn't he be glad.

2. Whenever I see a sparrow lyin'/ dead on a street,
   It re/minds me of him.
   Didn't he say his Father knew
   If/ even one fell
   And /doesn't he count every hair on your head.

3. Whenever I see a penny shining / bright in some child's hand,
   It re/minds me of him.
   Wouldn't he say that child gave all
   That he / had if he gave
   Just that / one little bit.

4. Whenever I see a bunch of grapes / purple on a vine,
   It re/minds me of him.
   Didn't he say our lives would be
   That/fruitful and alive,
   If / we lived in him.

5. Whenever I see a loaf of bread / fresh from the oven,
   It re/minds me of him.
   Didn't he give himself
   To / be our food,
   To / be our living bread.

6. Whenever I see a young man / smilin' at a bride,
   It re/minds me of him.
   Didn't he say we'd gather round
   A / banquet table of joy
   And / drink wine with him.

(In folk-song style, the syllables must be accommodated to fit the melody.
The diagonal line shows where the melody changes. The accent shows a rise
in pitch; underline, a lowering.)

APPENDIX

THIS TABLE SHOWS THE GENERAL DEVELOPMENT

B.C.	BIBLICAL HISTORY	
2000		
1850	Patriarchal Period	
	Abraham, Isaac, and Jacob	
1700	Hebrews in Egypt	
1300	Exodus under Moses	
	Conquest of Canaan under Josue	
1200	Period of the Judges	
1100		
1050	Philistine victory over Hebrews	
	Saul (1030-1010)	
1000	David (1010-970)	
	Solomon (970-931)	
950		
	Schism: Roboam and Jeroboam I	

B.C.	JUDA	ISRAEL
900		
850		Elia / Eliseus
800		Jeroboam II
750	Achaz Isaia	Amos and Osee
700	Ezechia Michea	Fall of Samaria
650	Josia	
	Jeremia	
600		
	Fall of Jerusalem	
550	Exile in Babylon	
	Ezechiel	
500	Return from Exile	
450	Ezra / Nehemia	
400		
350		
300	Hellenization	
250		
200	Antiochus IV	Pharisees
	Revolt of Maccabees	Sadducees
150	Qumran Community	Essenes
	Roman Domination	
100	Herod the Great	
50		
7-6	BIRTH OF JESUS CHRIST	

194

BOOKS OF THE OLD TESTAMENT · SECULAR HISTORY

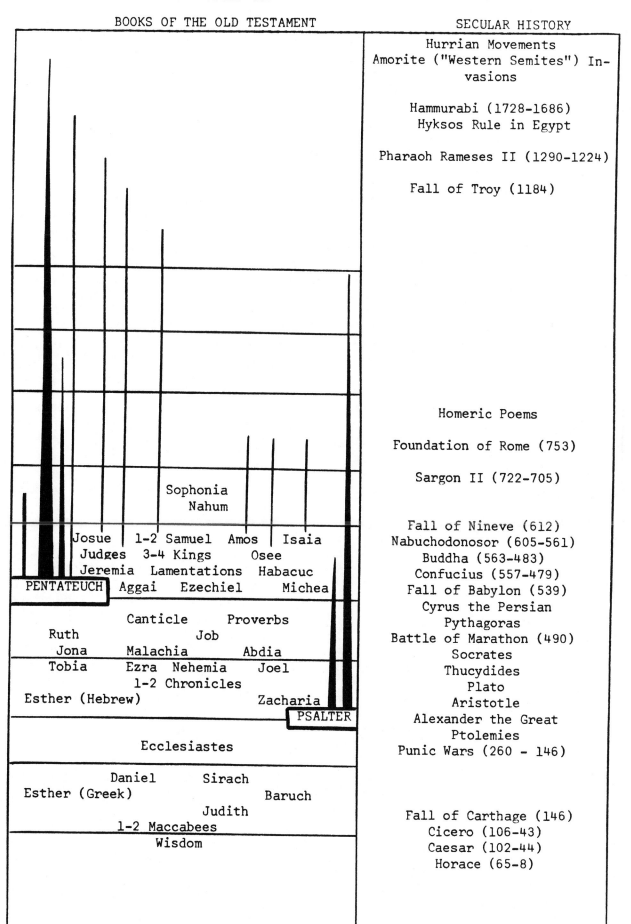

Hurrian Movements
Amorite ("Western Semites") Invasions

Hammurabi (1728-1686)
Hyksos Rule in Egypt

Pharaoh Rameses II (1290-1224)

Fall of Troy (1184)

Homeric Poems

Foundation of Rome (753)

Sargon II (722-705)

Fall of Nineve (612)
Nabuchodonosor (605-561)
Buddha (563-483)
Confucius (557-479)
Fall of Babylon (539)
Cyrus the Persian
Pythagoras
Battle of Marathon (490)
Socrates
Thucydides
Plato
Aristotle
Alexander the Great
Ptolemies
Punic Wars (260 - 146)

Fall of Carthage (146)
Cicero (106-43)
Caesar (102-44)
Horace (65-8)

Sophonia
Nahum

Josue   1-2 Samuel   Amos   Isaia
Judges   3-4 Kings   Osee
Jeremia Lamentations Habacuc
PENTATEUCH Aggai Ezechiel   Michea

Canticle   Proverbs
Ruth   Job
Jona   Malachia   Abdia
Tobia   Ezra Nehemia   Joel
1-2 Chronicles
Esther (Hebrew)   Zacharia
PSALTER

Ecclesiastes

Daniel   Sirach
Esther (Greek)   Baruch
Judith
1-2 Maccabees
Wisdom

It is a library, a collection of books written by many groups of men who lived at various times between 1250 B.C. and 100 A.D. These men were from all walks of life--priests, government officials, herdsmen, and fishermen. The original versions were in Hebrew, Aramaic, and Greek so that in their writings "God speaks in three languages."

A. The Table of Contents will help you locate the various books. The Old and the New Testament books may have duplicate numbering of the pages.

B. Some books have more than one volume; e.g., the Books of Kings. The number in front of the name always indicates the volume. Do not confuse Ecclesiastes and Ecclesiasticus, and the Gospel and the Epistle of St. John.

C. Some books have two names and some names have two spellings. Cf. list that follows.

D. Biblical references are usually given in this order: chapter number, colon, verse number.

John 12:1	refers to a single verse
John 12:1-7	refers to a series of consecutive verses
John 12:1,3,6	refers to a series of non-consecutive verses

BOOKS OF THE BIBLE--OLD TESTAMENT

NAME	ABBREVIATION	CONTENT

Pentateuch--Torah or Books of the Law

Genesis	Gn.	Traditional stories of creation and the Patriarchs
Exodus	Ex.	Account of the Hebrew liberation from Egyptian slavery and of the covenant
Leviticus	Lv.	Code of religious and civil laws
Numbers	Nu.	Account of forty years in the desert
Deuteronomy	Dt.	Religious reflections attributed to Moses

The Deuteronomist History

Joshua (Josue)	Jos.	Account of conquest of the Promised Land
Judges	Jgs.	Life in the Promised Land before the monarchy
4 Kings (2 Samuel, 2 Kings)	Kgs. Sm.	History of the monarchy
Ruth	Ru.	Story of a Moabite woman, an ancestor of Christ

The Chronicler History

2 Paralipomenon (2 Chronicles)	Par. Chr.	Additions to the royal period.
1 Esdras (Ezra)	Esd. (Ezr.)	Period of reconstruction after the return from exile
2 Esdras (Nehemias)	Neh.	
2 Maccabees	Mc.	Account of the religious revolt against paganism

Didactic Midrash

Baruch	Bar.	Instruction on the proper dispositions with which the Israelites are to make the annual pilgrimage to Jerusalem.
* Tobias	Tb.	Descriptive narrative of ideal family life
Jonah	Jon.	Satire on the narrow nationalism and intolerance of fifth century Jews
* Esther	Est.	Story of a Hebrew woman's dedication to her people

Apocalyptic Literature

* Judith	Jt.	Story of heroic trust in Yahweh that should characterize the nation
Joel	Jl.	Two sermons calling upon people to pray and do penance to avert calamity
* Daniel	Dn.	Written to encourage the persecuted faithful to resist Antiochus and his pagan culture

Poetry

Psalms	Ps.	Collection of prayers and liturgical songs
Canticle of Canticles (Song of Songs)	Ct.	Wedding song, typifying Yahweh's love for Israel

Books of Wisdom

Job	Jb.	Drama dealing with the problem of the sufferings of the innocent
Proverbs	Prv.	Collection of moral sayings for the young
Ecclesiastes (Qoheleth)	Eccl.	Reflections on life and death
* Wisdom	Wis.	Reflections on Jewish ideals and values
* Ecclesiasticus (Sirach)	Ecclus. Sir.	Outline of moral training and religious education

* - Called "Apocryphal" by Jews and Protestants

NAME	ABBREVIATION

Prophetical Books

Prophets of Judah

Isaiah	Is.
Sophoniah (Zephaniah)	So.
Nahum	Na.
Ezechiel	Ez.
Abdiah (Obdiah)	Abd.
Micheah (Micah)	Mi.
Jeremiah	Jer.
Habacuc (Habakkuk)	Hb.
Lamentations	Lam.

Prophets of Israel

Amos	Am.
Osee (Hosea)	Os.

Post-Exilic Prophets

Aggai (Aggeus)	Ag.
Zachariah	Za.
Malachiah	Mal.

BOOKS OF THE BIBLE--NEW TESTAMENT

Gospels

Matthew	Mt.
Mark	Mk.
Luke	Lk.
John	Jn

Acts of the Apostles

	Acts

Apocalypse

	Ap.

Epistles

Colossians	Col.
1 Corinthians	1 Cor.
2 Corinthians	2 Cor.
Ephesians	Eph.
Galatians	Gal.
Hebrews	Heb.
James	Jas.
1 John	1 Jn.
2 John	2 Jn.
3 John	3 Jn.
Jude	Jude
1 Peter	1 Pt.
2 Peter	2 Pt.
Philemon	Phl.
Philippians	Phil.
Romans	Rom.
1 Thessalonians	1 Thes.
2 Thessalonians	2 Thes.
1 Timothy	1 Tm.
2 Timothy	2 Tm.
Titus	Ti.

B 7
C 8
D 9
E 0
F 1
G 2
H 3
I 4
J 5